THE GUIDE FOR INCLUSIVE LEADERS

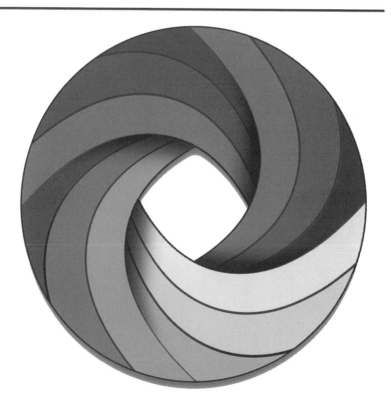

PUBLISHED BY:
PRINCETON TRAINING PRESS
PRINCETON, NEW JERSEY

a TMC Company
600 Alexander Road
Princeton, New Jersey 08540-6011 USA

Tel: 609-951-0525
Fax: 609-951-0395
Web: www.tmcorp.com
E-mail: info@tmcorp.com

Editor-in-Chief: Tim Walker
Cover Design/Illustrations: Miguel Roman
Layout: Eric Charbonneau

ISBN: 1-882390-33-4

Table of Contents

Preface

This Guide is the result of a quest to develop a globally consistent and locally relevant approach to help managers and leaders everywhere address the increasing challenges of diversity and inclusion in their sphere of influence. We embarked on a worldwide exploration of issues and concerns to discover that the incredible variety of issues and concerns we had the privilege to learn about had a simple common theme. Each unique case revealed that our organizations as much as our societies are riddled by the human tendency to organize in- and out-groups, and to develop cultural norms around them. We carefully validated this insight and along the way developed the skills, tools and frameworks introduced in this Guide.

It soon became evident that what we discovered had applications beyond a narrow understanding of diversity and relevance to a spectrum of important business challenges, such as innovation, corporate mergers and acquisitions, and cross-functional teamwork. In each case, inclusion is an important requirement for success, yet difficult to attain. To aid those managers and leaders not being trained to enable inclusion, developing specific guidelines became an important undertaking.

This Guide summarizes the insights we gained and hopefully provides useful framework, tools and action recommendations that can transform unproductive situations and relations for mutual benefit, growth and success.

We are most grateful to the many participants, sponsors of workshops, and focus groups conducted around the world. Special thanks to: Leticia Knowles of American Express, Michelle Goad of ArvinMeritor, Lesley Billow of Volvo Trucks, Dorian Baroni of BP, Nerys Wadham of Novartis, Margret Schweer of Kraft Foods, Jorge Mesquita and Keith Lawrence of Procter & Gamble, Cindy Zimmerer and Bill Manfredi of Young & Rubicam Brands, Magda Nowak of Pepsico International, Geraldine M. Bown of Domino Perspectives and Donna Stringer of Executive Diversity Services.

At IBM we are particularly thankful to John (Ted) Childs, Jr., Vice President, Global Workforce Diversity, Hans Ulrich Maerki, Chairman of the Board Europe, Claudia Woody, Managing Director, D.J. Nyamane, Director, Johannesburg South Africa, and Larry Hirst, General Manager, UK.

At TMC, we would like to thank Esther Lewis, Angela Yen, Alina Enggist, Eric Charbonneau, and Tim and Danielle Walker for their work and support in crafting this approach.

Joerg Schmitz is deeply grateful to his wife, Latha, and daughter, Christina, for their love, support, inspiration and ideas. Special thanks also to his father, Helmut P. Schmitz who has significantly inspired Joerg's interest in the issues of diversity, multiculturalism and inclusion.

Nancy Curl gives gratitude for her father, James B. Swatzell, who provides her unconditional love on which all success is based. Special appreciation and love to Wayne, Evelyn, Derek, Marilyn and Alex for their encouragement and inspiration as role models for inclusion.

CHAPTER 1

Inclusive Leadership – A Global Dynamic

The challenges, developments and trends in societies, marketplaces and workforces worldwide create a spectrum of new risks and opportunities. Seizing these opportunities and reducing the risks requires specific awareness, knowledge, skills and actions which we associate with *Inclusive Leadership*.

Inclusive leaders set, model and reinforce standards and practices that enable individuals and groups to contribute to their fullest potential by leveraging their unique abilities, experiences, perspectives and viewpoints for the collective benefit of all stakeholders. Inclusive Leadership is a vehicle for improving and/or changing both micro and macro levels of human interaction, collaboration and organization to achieve greater cohesion, trust, motivation, creativity, inspiration, satisfaction and commitment.

This guide is a learning resource for developing the core competency of inclusive leadership – a seemingly "soft" aspect upon which success and performance so critically depend in this complex, diverse and interconnected world.

Shared values and norms among people afford us the luxury of leaving these "soft" aspects largely outside of concentrated attention and thorough exploration. With the dynamic changes in our social, cultural, economic, business, professional and organizational realities, there is increased fragmentation and diversity in values and norms that reveal these "soft" aspects to be some of the hardest and most essential ingredients of success. Precisely because they necessitate attention to, and exploration of, areas of human perception, interaction, and behavior, their relation to performance is rarely questioned and even less often discussed.

◼ Global Trends and Developments

A number of trends and developments exist on a global level. Consider the effect of each on society, organizations and workplaces:

1. The workforce in developed and developing economies is getting older as a direct outcome of population aging.

Consider the following:

- Population aging is a phenomenon that the worldwide population is currently experiencing

- While the size of the older population segment is growing both in absolute and relative terms, the size of the younger segment is shrinking

- Throughout history, the population of those aged 60 and over has never been more than five percent of the total population of any country

- Today, the population share of the elderly has been steadily rising for the past century. In the developed world, 20% of the population is at least 60 years of age. By 2040, almost 35% (50% in some countries) of the developed world's population will be aged 60 or older

- Several countries—including China, Taiwan and Singapore—are projected to approach developed-world levels of elderly population percentages by the middle of this century

- Businesses and organizations will be affected by:
    - Higher taxes, rising capital costs, shrinking consumer markets and falling tangible assets and equity valuations

    - Tightening labor markets will make it difficult to retain top talent

    - Overcapacity in real estate, construction, retail and other key sectors

- Intensified competition over shrinking sales, which will reduce returns on investment and...

- Possibly generate new pressures for capital controls, non-tariff barriers and outright protectionism

2. The percentage of immigrants and minorities in the workforce of industrialized countries will increase.

Consider the following:

- The projected changes in labor markets, as a result of population aging, create strong incentives to recruit foreigners or move production to countries that are less developed and have younger populations

- Many countries have made targeted efforts to attract foreigners to study and work in their countries

- Countries that have historically not been 'immigrant countries' have begun to attract immigrants

- The immigration trends increase the linguistic, ethnic and/or religious fragmentation and diversity in traditionally more homogeneous societies

- The ability to attract and retain immigrant talent is an emerging source of competitiveness

3. The proportion of women in the workforce and in decision-making positions will increase.

Consider the following:

- Women have participated increasingly in the labor force worldwide, enabling them to achieve their potential in the labor market and to attain economic independence in many parts of the world

- Women are entering the global labor force in record numbers

- In 2003, 1.1 billion (about 40%) of the world's 2.8 billion workers were women. This represents a worldwide increase of nearly 200 million women over a ten year span

- Improved equality in terms of the number of male and female workers has yet to result in (1) real socioeconomic empowerment for most women, (2) equal pay for work of equal value and (3) gender balance across occupations or within executive ranks

- Women face higher unemployment rates, lower wages and represent 60% of the world's 550 million working poor

- Women work 2/3 of the world's working hours and produce half of the world's food, yet earn only ten percent of the world's income and own less than one percent of the world's property

4. People with disabilities require integration into the workforce.

Consider the following:

- The World Health Organization estimates that over 600 million people, or ten percent of the world's population, have a disability

- Disability is falsely regarded as an obstacle to work and equated with severe handicaps such as visual, hearing and mobility problems and impairments which require substantial aid and workplace adjustments

- Of the working-age disabled in the *Organisation for Economic Co-operation and Development* (OECD) countries, only about 1/3 are affected by severe disabilities

- The majority of people with disabilities suffer from stress-related, muscular and cardiovascular diseases

- Mental and psychological disabilities are on the rise

- As a result of the aging population, age-related disabilities are increasing

- People with disabilities are often capable and willing to participate actively in social and economic opportunities

5. Life - Balance / Work Flexibility (health conditions, dependent care obligations).

Consider the following:

- Long-term trends in the labor market indicate an increase in both divorce rates and the proportion of parents at work. The increase in dual-earner families and lone-parent families where the parent is working results in a growing proportion of the workforce heavily involved in family life and responsibilities

- Flexible work options are and will continue to be important responses to additional changes and requirements:

    - The increasing time squeeze between work and home

    - The organizational benefits of implementing a range of flexible work options

    - The importance of developing and maintaining a diverse, skilled and motivated workforce

    - Workforce demographics (aging of the population leading to dependent care)

    - The increasing demand for immediate and constant client services, including times outside of normal business hours

    - The increasing emphasis on leisure time

    - Need to combat skill obsolescence through continuing education and training

6. Increasing acceptance and recognition of gays and lesbians.

Consider the following:

- The social and legal meaning of marriage varies across culture, time, and space

- In the context of gay and lesbian rights, marriage refers to the legal union between two people recognized by the state and is subject to the rights, benefits and obligations prescribed by that state

- In the last fifteen years South Africa, Australia, New Zealand, Argentina, Canada, certain cities in Italy, Hawaii, Vermont in the US, and a number of countries in Europe have granted legal recognition to same-sex partnerships or civil unions

- "Registered partnership," or civil union, is a model of quasi-marriage pioneered by the Scandinavian countries of Norway, Sweden, Iceland and the Netherlands which grants most of the protection and anti-discrimination rights to homosexual couples that are equal to that of heterosexual couples

- In a few additional countries same-sex unions are recognized and applied to limited fields such as inheritance, immigration and job benefits

- Asian, Middle Eastern and African states generally have strong discriminatory treatment of gays and lesbians in society, culture and law

7. Accelerating gap between rich and poor populations.

Consider the following:

- More than four billion people live on less than $2 USD per day; an additional 1.5-1.7 billion live on $25 USD or less

- Traditional logic of many multinational corporations has not integrated the poor as a serious potential market, in spite of analyses and experiences to the contrary

- Poverty and economic disenfranchising are contributing factors to both ethnic and social tensions, as well as political and economic instability

- Developing countries offer significant growth and resource opportunities

- The poor consume; although consumption patterns require innovation and creativity on behalf of multinational companies who seek to cater to them

- The poor have attractive aggregate purchasing power

- The poor have a lot to gain from new technologies and adopt it readily

8. More frequent interactions between people of diverse national, linguistic, cultural and ethnic backgrounds.

Consider the following:

- 50 of the top 100 economies in the world are global corporations

- These corporations are economically more powerful than most nation states or political bodies

- They typically operate in 120 to 150 countries connecting a diverse web of ethnically, linguistically and culturally diverse customers/consumers, employees and suppliers

9. Cross-functional synergy as well as effective collaboration and knowledge management/transfer are the drivers of competitive advantage in complex global matrix organizations.

Consider the following:

- Differences by functional culture are as strong, if not stronger, than national cultures and require similar skills to be bridged effectively

- Matrix organizations have effectively shifted the risk from "hard" to "soft" variables, identifying ineffective communication, knowledge transfer and collaboration as prime risk factors

- Effective knowledge and innovation processes are at the heart of competitiveness in the global economy

10. Environmental Responsibility and Conservationism.

Consider the following:

- The environmental impact of global corporations is increasingly scrutinized by both government and non-governmental organizations

- Consumers' perceptions of a corporation's environmental record impact its brand positioning and profitability

- Corporations that anticipate and meet environmental standards before they become legally binding have an advantage over organizations that need to make abrupt and often costly adjustments in a short span of time

Of course, the above list is not exhaustive. It certainly does not include all of the specific issues that exist on regional and/or local levels. These developments mean that differences and concerns previously considered distant, hidden and irrelevant are fast becoming relevant to organizations and their managers.

Increasing legislation and regulation worldwide concerning some of these issues is evidence that this awareness is spreading quickly and that companies, organizations and individuals need to seriously consider their impact.

Hidden in the above trends are risks, opportunities and challenges. The increasing global interconnectedness with its tremendous diversity, heterogeneity and complexity suddenly force them into our awareness.

But aside from legal mandates, if the inherent risks, challenges and opportunities are left unexplored, we may not only miss out on competitive advantage, but contribute to the worsening of the human condition. The awareness of diversity brings with it a very personal demand to introspect and transforms our model of the world, the assumptions upon which we operate and the motivation of our actions and decisions.

Exploration Exercise 1:

Review the above trends and challenges and consider the following:

o   How is your organization affected by these trends? Which ones are most important?

o   How are these recognized and addressed currently?

o   How is your team (or your teams) affected by these trends? How well does your team respond to them? (be specific)

o   How do these trends and challenges affect you personally? (be specific)

o   What have you done/can you do to address these trends and challenges?

CHAPTER 2

What Inclusive Leadership Is All About

An individual's mental models are the primary limiting factor to achieving his or her full potential. In an organization, the business model and ingrained biases can be a limiting factor for the organization and its employees. Human diversity and the issues and challenges explored previously push the limits of both mental models and organizational biases to realize the full and best potential of individuals and organizations.

When done well it can improve performance at levels similar to Six Sigma, Total Quality, ERP, Lean and many others that have swept global enterprises. Each of these initiatives acts on a causal link between individual behavior, business processes and business results. Based on careful mapping and analysis, they yield prescriptions for behavioral and process changes. Productivity gains, expansion, growth and sometimes simply survival, justify the required investment of money, people and time.

Fundamental to effective *Inclusive Leadership* is the acceptance of a specific underlying worldview and value system. Individual leaders have to think through these values and determine the degree to which they expect their organization to model them.

- *Variance and variability from and non-conformance with the social norm are positive and need to be encouraged –* Social norms pervade societies and organizations. Diversity and Inclusion work is built on the belief that static and unchallenged social norms stifle creativity and innovation, create complacency and ultimately hinder agility and adaptability. Ensuring that diversity of thought, opinions, experiences and perspectives are represented within an organization is often the essential breeding ground for innovation and growth.

- *Freedom from discrimination is a universal right, including at work.* Not unrelated to the first value, Diversity and Inclusion is rooted in a stance of discrimination-free, fair and equitable labor practices. This set of beliefs is probably best articulated by the Declaration of Fundamental Principles and Rights at Work, formulated by the United Nation's International Labour Organization (ILO).[1]

- *Meritocracy and individual performance orientation are the only permissible standards within an organization.* This is the conviction that only the performance related skills of individuals should determine their success in an organization. In recruitment, selection, promotion and the terms and conditions of work only individual merit- and skill-related aspects are relevant.

- *Business success rests on future-oriented strategic planning.* To ensure the continuing competitive health of an organization, change may be required today. Foresight now prepares an organization to lead in the future when business conditions may be radically different. Projections and trends must be carefully tracked to determine their potential impact and specific actions taken to position the business in a leading position. The profound consequences of demographic trends that are projected to affect both the workforce and consumer base will force many organizations to rethink policies, strategies, products and services.

- *Companies need to prove themselves as Ethical and Responsible Corporate Citizens to grow and survive.* In particular, global companies need to become good local citizens that understand the needs of their customers and value the communities from which they derive profit. The reputation for being a responsible agent within the community has positive impact on public perception and appeal as an employer, securing the company's longevity in the given market.

Examples

o BMW relies significantly on the participation of customers/consumers for their innovative new product development efforts.

o P&G offers qualifying domestic partners health care, family life insurance, long-term care insurance, and surviving spouse benefits.

o IBM proactively partners with governments and consults in the establishment of diversity and inclusion related legislation, requirements and guidelines.

o Deloitte gives parents the flexibility to manage their dependent care responsibilities. (Many companies create and encourage specific flexible work arrangements for employees with dependent care responsibilities.)

o BP has actively cultivated a "green," environmentally responsible corporate image.

o Hyperion offers its employees financial incentives for electing to purchase hybrid automobiles.

o Bank of America has developed a comprehensive skill building initiative for its mortgage representatives to penetrate ethnic markets.

o CEMEX of Mexico and AMUL of India have developed business models addressing the need for empowerment of poor segments of the population.

o PepsiCo International actively seeks to employ disabled workers for Quality Assurance in Mexico and Brazil. This initiative has significantly contributed to superior results and improved employee morale and loyalty.

o Nike recycles sneakers to create sport surfaces in communities in which the residents typically do not have access to high-performance sports surfaces.

- o GE publishes a citizenship report in which it outlines its work in the community, its environmental, health and safety performance as part of a commitment to greater transparency to their community contributions.

- o Citigroup, Bank Rakyat Indonesia, ICICI Bank of India and ACCION International are examples of financial institutions with specific microfinance strategies and programs creating access, opportunities and empowerment for some of the world's poorest populations.

Exploration Exercise 2:

Review the core beliefs and values represented above and:

- o Assess the strength with which you share these values. The ones that resonate strongest will probably define your personal affinity and focus of your inclusive leadership.

- o To what degree does your organization believe in and support these principles? Identify examples of your company's initiatives and involvement with stakeholder communities.

- o How can your business benefit from acting on these beliefs and principles?

- o What are you willing to do in your sphere of influence?

■ The Power of Inclusive Leadership

Inclusive Leaders combine support of the aforementioned value system with their commitment to results. They understand the full and constructive power that resides in:

- what she/he pays attention to, measures and controls

- how she/he reacts to critical incidents and crises

- what she/he teaches and coaches

- what she/he models and demonstrates

- how she/he allocates rewards and recognition

- what criteria she/he uses to recruit, select and promote employees, partners and contractors

Inclusive leaders apply these levers mindfully and with the intent to:

a) realize the hidden power of differences,
b) overcome barriers created by differences and/or reactions to them,
c) embed practices and standards for managing and leveraging differences in the organization culture.

Their actions create and foster a quality of inclusiveness within the organization that is necessary to turn diversity into an organizational asset.

Diversity is a given, Inclusion is an option

Global organizations are characterized by a high level of diversity, particularly on a linguistic, cultural (national, organizational and functional) and experiential basis. What is not a given, however, is the degree to which the organization's culture possesses the quality of inclusiveness. Organizations that understand this and focus on developing and supporting inclusion through committed and supportive "inclusive leaders" will have the edge.

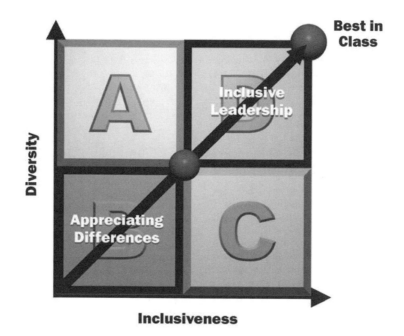

Illustration 2.1: Diversity and Inclusion Force Field

ABOUT THE DIVERSITY AND INCLUSION FORCE FIELD

Quadrant A describes a situation in which an organization exhibits a lot of diversity, but has not managed to develop a culture and climate capable of supporting and sustaining it. Shared practices and processes are missing that accommodate the diverse and complex needs and unleash the inherent potential. Such an organization is characterized by a "closed culture," requiring adaptation to a narrow success profile and/or difficulties attracting and retaining diverse talent.

Organizations in **Quadrant B** are characterized by moderate degrees of diversity accompanied by a moderately "open culture". Such organizations are able to retain their current levels of diversity, but may encounter significant difficulties attracting and retaining a more diverse workforce; i.e., keeping pace with the trends and developments.

Organizations in **Quadrant C** exhibit an "open culture", i.e., formal policies and systems and informal practices that are capable of sustaining and leveraging a wide spectrum of workforce diversity. However, these organizations have not managed to attract or retain a diverse workforce.

Quadrant D characterizes organizations that have managed to support and leverage a wide spectrum of workforce diversity through an "open culture" that is characterized by inclusive policies, processes, systems and practices. These are actively fostered, reviewed and refined by managers at all levels of the organization.

Focusing on the behaviors and practices that enable inclusion (i.e., enable organizations to operate in quadrant D) provides an applicable framework independent of the specific sources of difference. As such, Inclusive Leadership is not limited to workforce demographics or what is referred to as "primary dimensions" of diversity (gender, age, ethnicity/race, nationality, language, disability, etc.). It applies equally to differences in thinking styles, personality, functional/occupational cultures, location, organizational culture (merger/acquisition), etc.

Inclusive Leadership focuses on the following commonalities of diversity issues, namely:

- exclusion or inequitable treatment and consideration of individuals or groups based on attributes *other than* skill, merit, qualification or past performance

- impact of unproductive effects of the exclusion – i.e., individuals or group does not contribute to their fullest potential. Creativity and innovation capabilities are lost, morale decreases, recruitment, retention, and representation are hindered, as well as market and growth opportunities missed

Exploration Exercise 3:

o Where do you see your organization, business unit and team positioned in the Diversity and Inclusion Force Field? Place a mark in the quadrant you think best describes the current state.

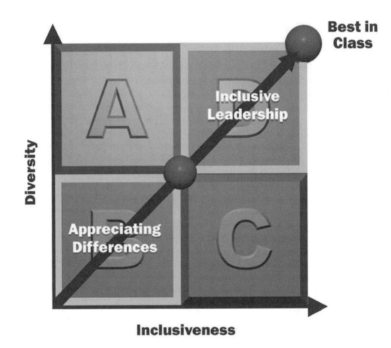

o What made you decide on this positioning?

o Are the positions different for the various issues and challenges (such as gender, people with disabilities, ethnicity)?

◗ Developing Inclusive Leadership

Inclusive leaders propel their team and organizations into Quadrant D of the Diversity and Inclusion Force Field. They develop specific awareness, knowledge, skills and take action in their spheres of influence. There are three developmental steps:

Step 1: Appreciate Differences
This step consists of building awareness for human differences, their origins, and impact on interactions, teamwork, culture and performance.

Step 2: Identify and Transform Exclusion Behaviors
This step consists of applying the gained awareness to the specific exclusion behaviors and patterns in one's sphere of influence. Actions include perfecting and applying a variety of tools and skills, including the ability to facilitate constructive conversations.

Step 3: Embed Inclusion Practices into the Culture
This step consists of specific actions that institutionalize inclusive practices in the organization. These actions facilitate an environment in which differences can flourish and are leveraged for the benefit of all stakeholders.

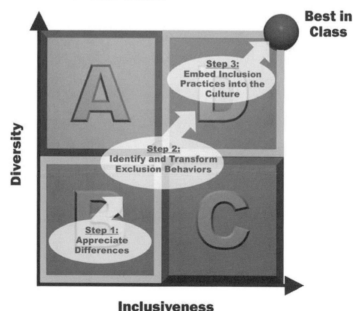

Illustration 2.2: The Development of Inclusive Leadership

CHAPTER 3

STEP 1: Appreciate Differences

This first step involves creating awareness and appreciation for human differences – their nature, their origins, and their impact on interactions, teamwork and performance.

Each individual operates with a distinct *Frame of Reference* which she/he shares to varying degrees with others. An individual's Frame of Reference can be understood as his or her system of meaning manifested in both visible and invisible aspects of her/his being.

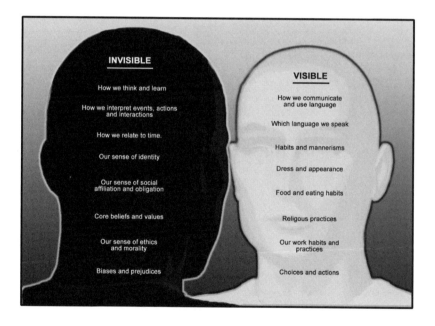

Illustration 3.1: Frame of Reference

This concept assumes that outwardly visible elements of an individual or a group are reflections of an internal set of attitudes, beliefs, assumptions, values, etc. A frame of reference therefore significantly influences how we perceive, evaluate and relate to others.

The aspects highlighted in Illustration 3.1 are not exhaustive and others can be added. It is however important to realize the invariable relationship between invisible and visible aspects. Whatever our attitudes, beliefs, assumptions, biases, prejudice and values, they find expression on the visible level[2]. The invisible aspects determine how we perceive, act and react to others, to situations and events. They have significant impact regarding what/who we like and prefer, what/who we feel indifferent about, and what/who we dislike and reject.

These three basic reactions to people and/or situations can be simplistically likened to a thermostat.

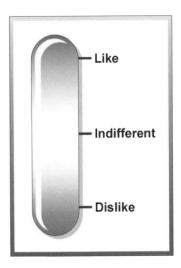

When we react to people along these three categories, we need to realize our tendencies to:

- overlook or excuse negative attributes or performance and exaggerate positives of those we like

- not notice or ignore the positive attributes or performances of those about which we feel indifferent

- exaggerate negative attributes or performance and minimize positives of those we dislike

It is critical that we understand the relation between our reaction and behavior to others, their performance and success. We need to clearly recognize the subjective standards we apply based on our Frame of Reference.

Frame of Reference Exploration

1. What are some of your preferences, core beliefs, values, and biases (invisibles)? (*e.g., timeliness and punctuality, formal interactions, prefer highly educated colleagues, etc.*)

2. What have you learned about yourself, your frame of reference, and its effect in interactions? Identify insights gained from any of the following sources.

Personality Assessments (e.g., Myers-Briggs Type Indicator, DISK,...)	
Management Style Assessments (e.g., Thomas Kilman Conflict Mode, Decision-Making Style, ...)	
Cultural/Inclusiveness Profiles (e.g., Cultural Orientations Indicator®, Inclusive Leadership Profile,....)	
360° Feedback and/or Performance Feedback	
Other:	

Your Autobiographical Snapshot

Through the previous exploration, you have sketched something similar to an autobiographical snapshot. We are likely to uncover a complex relationship between aspects that are out of our control (that are to some degree biologically determined), aspects that are socially/culturally determined, and aspects that are associated with the choices and experiences of the individual.

As important as it is to develop awareness of one's Frame of Reference, it may be as instructive to explore the factors that have influenced its development.

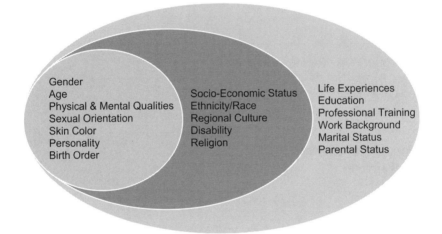

Gender
Age
Physical & Mental Qualities
Sexual Orientation
Skin Color
Personality
Birth Order

Socio-Economic Status
Ethnicity/Race
Regional Culture
Disability
Religion

Life Experiences
Education
Professional Training
Work Background
Marital Status
Parental Status

Illustration 3.2: Factors Influencing Our Frame of Reference

This illustration depicts the three types through concentric circles. The aspects to the left are those out of individual or social/cultural control, in the center aspects under social/cultural control, and to the right those related to individual choices and experiences.

For example, 'race' is a classification of people often based upon certain physical characteristics such as skin color. Yet types of races or racial categories are specific to a given social or cultural group. For example, race is an important social category in the United States and in South Africa. However, the U.S. recognizes Blacks or African-American and White/Caucasian, whereas South Africa distinguishes between Blacks, Coloreds and Whites. These labels are related to specific histories and cultural viewpoints. Ethnicity, religion and what constitutes a disability and what does not are equal reflections of a specific society or culture (under social/cultural control).

Reflection

How do the aspects that are out of your individual or social/cultural control affect you (perhaps in ways that you have never considered before)?

Practice Scenarios

Identify the Frames of Reference, values and mindsets that may apply in the following scenarios:

1. Delegation *

You are a recent expatriate responsible for managing customer support. After transferring to your new assignment, you felt first hand the negative reactions of some local male managers to your role as a female leader. You want to change the environment to be more welcoming for other women. You are acutely aware that you are in a different culture and want to be sensitive to those differences, including styles of communication and personal interactions.

You have one female manager reporting to you. She is the least experienced on your team. You want to make sure that she succeeds and have carefully selected assignments that offer her experience but little risk of failure. You are grooming her for a possible division assignment. You have talked to her formally and informally about her job and career. She is always positive and likes her work.

However, you have a sense that she is not really happy. You think she might not be giving you direct feedback due to cultural reasons. You have also picked up some signs that male colleagues think you're being too easy with your female manager.

2. She is hurting your career! *

You report to a female expatriate. You expected that, being a woman, she would be supportive of your career. However, you are receiving mixed messages from her. On one hand, she spends time with you and states she is supportive of your career aspirations. Yet, she has tended to give key assignments to your male colleagues and relegated you to less important accounts. This is hurting your career and reinforces some people's views of the work women should do and their lesser qualification.

You have indicated your dissatisfaction to your manager in indirect, very respectful ways. Unfortunately, she doesn't seem to understand. You want to communicate your needs to her, but you also do not want to upset her. After all, she is your boss and can make or break your career. Is she trying to help you or sabotage your career?

*NOTE: While these examples use "women" any number of other identifiers may be substituted such as "disabled, gay, older or younger workers, etc.

Reflection

What aspects of your own frame of reference influence your behavior regarding team assignments, delegation, and promotions?

CHAPTER 4

STEP 2: Identify and Transform Exclusion Behaviors

This step takes the appreciation of differences one step further. Our Frame of Reference, particularly when socially reinforced, contributes to a situation of inclusion or exclusion. After identifying the mechanisms that create exclusion and the inherent risks and cost of exclusion, we can foster inclusion in our sphere of influence. This includes applying a variety of tools and skills, including the ability to facilitate constructive conversations.

Divergent *Frames of Reference* either by groups or individuals can often result in inequitable treatment or consideration of individuals or groups based on aspects *other than* merit, skill, qualification, experience, point of view, past performance or potential contribution. Such a situation, when sustained over a period of time will trigger a social dynamic with undesirable and negative effects on the individuals, the organization, and potentially business performance. We have simplistically called this the "***insider-outsider dynamic.***"

In the workplace and within an organization, this dynamic can lead to sub-optimal performance and low employee satisfaction and commitment. This dynamic causes the talents and insights needed to respond to marketplace challenges to remain hidden, internal conflict to divert needed energy and attention from the marketplace and customers, and erode performance and potential over time.

Managers/leaders need to be prepared to identify and transform exclusive behaviors in their sphere of influence. This ability requires the following knowledge and skills:

- Understanding exclusion and the associated risks and opportunities

- Identifying specific behavior and reaction patterns in response to these dynamics

- Change exclusion behaviors through coaching and/or feedback

- Engage in Constructive Conversations (to address existing issues or prevent their future occurrence)

Each is considered in detail in the following sections.

Understanding Exclusion, its Risks and the Opportunities of Inclusion

Most people have an intuitive sense of what exclusion means. It is created through the emergence of *insiders* and *outsiders* in social situations. The predictable patterns in the interactions between them yield specific risks, costs, and opportunities. In fact, most know exactly what is meant by *insider* and *outsider* and what each feels like. This is partly a function of their ubiquitous nature in our social experience.

The labels of *insider* and *outsider*, as we use them, do NOT characterize people in the totality of their personal or professional lives. We apply these labels as descriptions for roles, perceptions and perspectives individuals assume depending on specific issues and situations. This means that each individual is both an insider and outsider depending on the situation, circumstance or context.

Insiders are individuals or groups who, in a given situation, circumstance or context:

- Have a formal and/or informal power to set the standards or rules for an entire group
- Set expectations and reinforce and reward compliant behavior
- Have the most to gain from the maintenance of established standards and rules

Outsiders are individuals or groups who, in a given situation, circumstance or context:

- Have little or no power to set standards and rules
- Are generally expected to adhere to the dominant expectations and standards
- Are put at a disadvantage: dominant standards minimize, curtail or prohibit their full contribution to a group

Outsider or *Insider* simply identifies the side of social power to which one belongs in given social situations.

Reflection

In which situations are you an insider or outsider?

Based on what?

How does each experience impact your ability to contribute?

The Interaction Patterns between Insiders and Outsiders

Before investigating the various reactions to being either an insider or outsider in a given situation, it is useful to be aware of some key aspects of their interaction:

1. Both insiders and outsiders approach, interpret and evaluate others/situations by applying their own Frame of Reference as "normal" or "most desirable." Differences in the Frame of Reference of others tend to be perceived from neutral to negative (either hot or cold).

2. Outsiders tend to be labeled negatively and stereotypical judgments are applied to them by insiders.

3. Insiders inadvertently and unconsciously communicate pressure to assimilate and conform to their standards and norms.

4. Outsiders tend to feel confused, vulnerable and comparatively weaker.

5. Both insiders and outsiders have a heightened sense of control and power when interactions take place in their home environment ("home advantage").

6. Outsiders are left to figure out the rules of the new culture on their own and receive feedback only when they make "mistakes."

7. Outsiders look for and rely on support from other outsiders regardless of whether they are similar or different from each other.

8. Conflicts, tensions and frustrations that arise from the insider/outsider dynamic are usually internalized and may suddenly erupt.

9. The experience of being an insider or outsider significantly affects our perception of and reaction to the other party in conflict situations.

Insiders' tend to:

- Focus on the intent rather than the impact of *their* actions

- Emphasize *individual* motivation

- Assume outsiders have a "Victim Mentality"

- Believe it is acceptable for change to take time

Outsiders' tend to:

- Focus on the impact and consequences of insiders' actions

- Emphasize pattern of behavior and "Group Dynamics"

- Assume systemic disadvantage

- Desire immediate change

10. Being an outsider may negatively affect performance, motivation and contributions.

11. The outsider perspective harbors potentially beneficial insights and impulses for change, innovation and growth; often overlooked or minimized by insiders.

12. Little or no time is spent discussing differences, perspectives or the experience of exclusion, nor its effect on business decisions and outcomes.

The above patterns describe common elements of the insider or outsider experience. Often the experiences of the outsider are more vivid and conscious than those of the insider.

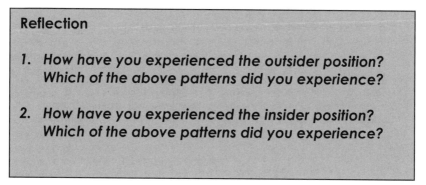

Reflection

1. *How have you experienced the outsider position? Which of the above patterns did you experience?*

2. *How have you experienced the insider position? Which of the above patterns did you experience?*

The Risks of Exclusion and Opportunities of Inclusion

While exclusion is a phenomenon rooted deeply in our individual and collective psychology, it harbors specific risks:

1. *Exclusion can foster overt and/or covert conflict and tension among individuals and groups.*

   Exclusion and inequitable treatment can create dissatisfaction and polarization. This can result in energies and attention being directed inwardly rather than outwardly. As a result, energies tend to be wasted on no-value added activities that maintain and fortify the exclusionary boundaries. The group or organization in question becomes stifled by inefficiency, lack of productivity, low motivation, commitment and loyalty.

2. *Exclusion can create backlash, requiring the dedication of resources to manage and contain them.*

   When exclusionary behaviors and practices are particularly oppressive (as can be observed in relations between ethnic, racial or religious groups throughout history), they can create the conditions for an equally oppressive backlash. The potential of a backlash requires the dedication of increasing amounts of resources to manage or suppress it. When a backlash does occur, it tends to unleash another cycle of exclusion, divisiveness, and backlash.

3. *Exclusion restricts adaptability and responsiveness by maintaining the status quo.*

   Exclusion requires the de-valuing of differences. Instead of perceiving them as an asset, they are considered a liability. This mindset jeopardizes the adaptability of a group or organization as its diversity constitutes the ultimate pool for creative and innovative potential. When exclusion is pronounced and variability discouraged, the group/ organization loses the ability to respond, grow, change and adapt to changing requirements, conditions and challenges.

Fostering inclusion is much like risk reduction and continuous improvement efforts. It seeks to actualize the following opportunities:

1. *Inclusion increases motivation, commitment, and loyalty*

When members of a group or organization are equally engaged, when they feel recognized, valued and an integral part of the group/organization, their motivation, commitment and loyalty increases commensurately. This reduces both soft and hard costs incurred by attrition, replacement, and the loss of productivity, effectiveness, and appeal.

2. Inclusion enables adaptability and responsiveness

Inclusion engages a wide and diverse group of individuals whose differences and attributes are seen as a competitive asset in a fast-changing dynamic marketplace or environment. A wide range of variability increases the pool of resources, solutions, experiences and insights required to meet new challenges.

3. Inclusion is a key enabler of innovation and creativity

Inclusion of outsider perspectives and experiences is a critical resource for stimulating innovation and creativity. Therefore, it is not only necessary to include divergent perspectives and experiences, but also protect them from assimilative pressures.

4. Improves focus on value and results

Inclusion reduces the risks described above which take away the focus from generating true value and results. Enhancing inclusion is a prudent action improving the value-stream of a group/organization.

Based on the above, the Inclusive Leader should analyze the risks inherent in the insider-outsider dynamic and the benefits for individuals, teams, groups and organizations associated with inclusion.

This analysis will bring into focus the specific goals and related success indicators associated with her/his practice of Inclusive Leadership. With those in mind, she/he is ready to identify and counter the specific behavior and interaction patterns that create and fortify exclusion.

A Note on Insider and Outsider Mindsets

The experience of being an insider or outsider in a given social context is strong and powerful. It affects the course of actions and interactions, creates synergies or institutionalizes differences.

It is very important to understand that repeated experience of being an outsider or insider by an individual or an entire social group instills a pervasive mindset in the individual and/or group. Even in the absence of any real exclusionary behavior, an individual or group will react and interact with the expectation of being excluded; i.e., they act from an outsider mindset.

Historical exclusion, such as discrimination, disadvantage or degradation of a social group invariably creates a specific frame of reference that is as sensitive to any signs of exclusion as it is likely to react to situations as if it were exclusionary. In other words, an individual may exhibit any of the outsider behavior and reaction patterns described in the following section without being truly excluded.

Please note that a similar yet less harmful pattern exists for those who have been historically on the inside.

■ Identifying specific behavior and reaction patterns in response to these dynamics

When individuals find themselves in the same insider or outsider position repeatedly different coping strategies can be observed. On each side the individual makes a particular choice about how to handle and cope with their experience. These choices reveal whether one (a) actively perpetuates the insider-outsider dynamic, (b) passively reinforces it or (c) acts as a catalyst for positive change:

1. **Passive reinforcement** happens through unconscious behavioral patterns that tend to maintain and even strengthen the insider/outsider division. This happens most often when the experience of insider or outsider has become deeply embedded in an individual's worldview.

2. **Active perpetuation** happens through behavior that fortifies and accentuates the perceived division between insiders or outsiders. This happens most often when an individual's sense of identity is linked to being an insider or outsider.

3. **Change agency** happens by converting awareness of both the dangers and opportunities embedded in the insider/outsider dynamic into specific actions yielding a change in attitudes, perceptions and interaction patterns between insiders and outsiders. The result is an inclusive environment within which differences are recognized, accepted, and leveraged.

It is a powerful skill to identify one's own behavior and that of others as reinforcing, perpetuating or changing the social dynamics and to become aware of the effects. Armed with this skill, one can apply a new understanding to the interactions and social dynamics at work. This in turn can powerfully contribute to constructively addressing stifling conflicts that can not only be observed in teams and organizations, but also increasingly within wider society. When applied consciously and strategically, this skill can help bring about new levels of contribution and motivation, enabling change, innovation and growth for organizations.

Each of the three reaction types has different manifestations for insiders and outsiders. These are described in detail on the following pages. Leaders need to understand these types and thoughtfully apply the understanding to their spheres of influence in order to act as change agents and inclusive leaders.

Illustration 4.1: Reaction Types

Outsiders   **Insiders**

PASSIVE REINFORCERS

The Assimilator   **The Avoider**
The Separatist   **The Unintentional Offender**

ACTIVE PERPETUATORS

The Fighter   **The Intentional Offender**

CATALYSTS FOR CHANGE

Outsider Change Agent   **Insider Change Agent**

PASSIVE REINFORCERS

Both insiders and outsiders can mutually reinforce each other. They therefore reinforce the *status quo* and strengthen the undesirable and often negative consequences.

The following outsider types tend to reinforce:

- **The Assimilator**
- **The Separatist**

The following insider types tend to reinforce:

- **The Avoider**
- **The Unintentional Offender**

The Assimilator

The assimilator acquiesces to the expectations of the insider group by adopting the features and behaviors of the dominant culture and minimizing her/his "different" characteristics. The assimilator may feel uncomfortable with her/his differences and expend significant energy adapting to the predominant norms to simply *"fit in."*[3]

Assimilators support an exclusive environment. By "blending in" she/he will not contribute her/his unique and relevant qualities, perspectives and viewpoints to the organization because they may not be considered acceptable by the dominant group. The value of her/his different perspectives and viewpoints is consequently lost to the organization. If the organizational culture and dominant expectations are too restrictive, the perceived unacceptability and expenditure of personal energy may result in declining motivation and morale.

Typical Behavior

The assimilator may:

- Show empathy and/or support for the concerns of outsiders in private, but rarely in public
- Over-emphasize the typical traits and behavioral attributes of the insider group
- Be cautious and guarded when discussing her/his personal life
- Stay silent when a derogatory remark or joke is made
- Deflect an insensitive comment or remark by changing the topic

The Effects

- *For that individual:* The individual is accepted by the *insider* group and feels validated as a member of the organization. However, the individual may operate with an increasing degree of internalized tension and energy expenditure as a result of the forced "adaptation"

- *For the workplace* A more homogeneous environment is created, and the *status quo* is supported

- *For the organization*: Potential insights, change and innovation that can be gained from her/his background, experiences and perspective may be limited, as the *outsiders* feel uncomfortable with their differences and minimize heterogeneity as much as possible

Reflections

Who in your environment might act/react as an assimilator? Based on what observation? What are the effects?

How do you act/react as an assimilator? Towards which issues and in what situations? What are the effects?

■ The Separatist

The separatist limits contact with the dominant group. Subgroups form in the organization, and they each try to remain separate from the larger group.

Because separatist *outsiders* are alienated yet self-confident about their distinct attributes and traits, they actively maintain the barrier between themselves and the dominant group. If left unchecked, the organization may become a fragmented environment lacking synergy and the ability to collaborate effectively.

Typical Behavior

The separatist may:

- Limit contact and team work with coworkers from the insider group

- Waste time on unnecessary activities designed solely to remove him/herself from the environment in which she/he feels uncomfortable

- Find reasons to not participate in meetings, conversations and other processes designed to create cohesion, integration and inclusion

- Limit the sharing of knowledge and experience to the minimum required

- Frequently emphasize the unique and distinct characteristics of her/his own group

- Nurture a separatist culture and identity with an outsider group

- Comment on the sense of being excluded and undervalued in one-on-one conversations

The Effects

- *For that individual*: The individual maintains a strong sense of identity and value by affirming her/his difference from the dominant group. Her/his role in the organization becomes defined by her/his distinctiveness rather than her/his abilities

- *For the workplace*: Absenteeism and high turnover are possible outcomes as the separatist feels excluded and de-motivated by being undervalued. Fortification of boundaries in the workplace results in a lack of information sharing, diminished teamwork, and an increase in latent tension or overt conflict

- *For the organization*: The organization fails to capitalize on the unique qualities that outsiders bring. It becomes either more homogeneous as separatists leave the organization or fragmented as separatist groups build and maintain cliques

Reflections

Who in your environment might act/react as a separatist? Based on what observation? What are the effects?

How do you act/react as a separatist? Towards which issues and in what situations? What are the effects?

The Avoider

The avoider is aware of biases in him/herself and others, but is reluctant to counter the inappropriate words and behaviors of others and him/herself. An avoider may be aware that certain comments, behaviors and practices are offensive, exclusionary or alienating to colleagues, but will typically not make an effort to improve the work environment.

Because of the passive support of the avoider, *status quo* is maintained, and the organization maintains a culture of exclusion. If unaddressed, the avoider may never voice her/his concern about the discrimination of which she/he is aware.

Typical behavior

The avoider may:
- Keep silent when hearing a discriminatory joke or remark despite disagreeing with it
- Not take a stand against discriminatory or offensive behaviors or practices
- Not be open with her/his manager when asked about discriminatory behaviors in the workplace
- Be fearful of changing the *status quo*
- Signal support for outsider concerns in private, but does not take action publicly

The Effects

- *For that individual*: Because the individual does not openly oppose the exclusion against outsiders, she/he can retain membership in the insider group while privately empathizing with outsiders

- *For the workplace*: Despite the avoider's awareness of biases in him/herself and others, her/his inaction reinforces discrimination and supports an exclusionary environment

- *For the organization*: The organization continues to be exclusive because the silence of the avoider reinforces the discriminatory practices. The organization fails to capitalize on the unique value of differences

Reflections

Who in your environment might act/react as an avoider? Based on what observation? What are the effects?

How do you act/react as an avoider? Towards which issues and in what situations? What are the effects?

The Unintentional Offender

The unintentional offender excludes and/or offends people in the organization because of their differences without being aware of it. She/he will typically speak or behave in ways that negatively affect people in her/his work environment because of lack of awareness.

Though not malicious, the unintentional offender's behavior supports a non-inclusive work culture. If unchecked, those excluded or offended will not feel comfortable contributing to an environment in which they are marginalized.

Typical Behavior

The unintentional offender may:

- Call others by a nickname without understanding how it is received

- Laugh at a discriminatory joke

- Agree with a manager's unfair decision to exclude a qualified candidate because of a disability or cultural difference

- Repeat idiomatic expressions and colloquialisms that may offend others

- Use language and expressions without reflecting on their implications

The Effects

- *For that individual*: By unintentionally reinforcing stereotypes, prejudices and exclusionary practices, this individual asserts and maintains membership and social alliances with the insider group

- *For the workplace*: The unintentional offender reinforces the *status quo*. She/he perpetuates the validity of the status difference and supports the boundaries between insiders and outsiders within her/his work environment

- *For the organization*: The unintentional offender creates organizational barriers to integrating differences in backgrounds, opinions and perspectives into work processes and practices that lead to innovation. The organization will not attract and retain diverse talent. The unintentional offender places the organization at risk for legal liabilities and a discredited image

Reflections

Who in your environment might act/react as an unintentional offender? Based on what observation? What are the effects?

How do you act/react as an unintentional offender? Towards which issues and in what situations? What are the effects?

ACTIVE PERPETUATORS

Passive Reinforcers tacitly strengthen and sanction the actions of active perpetuators. Active perpetuators are strongly invested in the ongoing insider-outsider dynamics. Their sense of identity is often deeply intertwined with the insider-outsider power distinction.

As an insider, the *Intentional Offender* acts as an active perpetuator.

As an outsider, the *Fighter* acts as an active perpetuator.

The Intentional Offender

The intentional offender is aware of her/his behavior and prejudices but, nevertheless, continues to exclude outsiders. The intentional offender typically knowingly makes discriminatory remarks and behaves in ways that exclude fellow colleagues. Her/his judgment will be based on disability or cultural, gender, race, age, sexual orientation or any other real or perceived difference.

If the offensive behavior is supported or not stopped at the onset, the organizational culture will become more exclusive — suppressing the creative energy that differences bring to the workplace.

Typical Behavior

The intentional offender may:

- Use an offensive joke to purposefully alienate others

- Refuse to work with a competent colleague because of her/his real or perceived difference

- Restrict recruiting, selection or staffing efforts to those with attributes of, or belonging to, social groups deemed acceptable

- Make derogatory statements about others based on their attributes, social or ethnic background or any other "unacceptable" characteristic

- Cultivate a small group of trusted individuals around him /herself

- Act indifferently or angrily to any discussion of diversity concerns or issues

The Effects

- _For that individual_: By reinforcing stereotypes, prejudices and exclusionary practices, this individual asserts, maintains and protects the power within and/or of an insider network

- _For the workplace_: She/he perpetuates the validity of categorizing people by differences and strengthens the boundaries between insiders and outsiders within the work environment

- *For the organization*: The effects of this type of behavior can be quite destructive in any organization. Colleagues feel discriminated against and have little incentive to contribute to a work environment which is hostile and exclusive. The organization will not attract and retain diverse talent, and the intentional offender will place the organization at risk for legal liabilities and a discredited image

Reflections

Who in your environment might act/react as an intentional offender? Based on what observation? What are the effects?

How do you act/react as an intentional offender? Towards which issues and in what situations? What are the effects?

The Fighter

The fighter actively and overtly resists the pressure to assimilate and opposes the restrictive expectations and norms enforced by the insider group. The fighter typically makes her/his unique and diverse characteristics the center of her/his sense of social identity. She/he has a heightened sensitivity to exclusion and operates with determination and drive to change the *status quo*.

Fighters may assume that an "attack mode" is the best way to protect her/his individuality. As such, she/he may demand urgent and radical change. The fighter is instrumental in bringing to the forefront critical issues associated with engrained social norms, standards and expectations. If sustained over a long period, the provocative style of a fighter may adversely affect the workplace and performance. Resulting tensions may fortify and attention may become focused on the work environment rather than on the work itself. This can reinforce the *status quo* which is opposite of the fighter's intention.

Typical Behavior

The fighter may:

- Operate with a sense of mission and zeal concerning her/his differences
- Be extremely alert to any situation or circumstance that can be interpreted as exclusionary or discriminatory
- Respond in a harsh manner to any comment that may have a negative connotation to the distinctive characteristics of her/his group
- Attribute malicious intent even to inadvertent and unintentional exclusionary behaviors and practices
- Frequently bring up conversations about her/his differences even in situations where such conversations are inappropriate
- Be impatient with a slow pace of change
- Be uncompromising

- Threaten to use formal legal or disciplinary recourses without first exploring underlying issues and concerns
- Be highly sensitive to group dynamics and frequently raise her/his concerns

The Effects

- *For that individual*: The individual's sense of identity, linked to "resisting" dominant insiders, is validated and nurtured. The individual has a sense of purpose. However, the individual may become isolated from many colleagues as people are uncomfortable speaking around him/her for fear of any misunderstanding.

- *For the workplace*: Though the fighter helps to identify critical issues, over time she/he may contribute to a hostile atmosphere that leads to counterproductive results (e.g., fortified boundaries, increasing resentment between and within *insider* and *outsider* groups and reinforced stereotypes). This may result in diminished openness to diversity inclusion.

- *For the organization*: Too much focus is placed on internal power struggles rather than on overall performance and/or external clients. If the root cause of the problem remains hidden and unaddressed, performance will continue to decline and the work environment will become increasingly fractious.

Reflections

Who in your environment might act/react as a fighter? Based on what observation? What are the effects?

How do you act/react as a fighter? Towards which issues and in what situations? What are the effects?

CATALYSTS OF CHANGE

Passive Reinforcers and active perpetuators essentially form a powerful alliance. Changing the situation and averting undesirable and negative consequences requires a mindset and behavioral approach that can withstand the social power of this alliance. This mindset must be complemented with sensitivity, tact and focus that win over minds and hearts in support of positive change.

These individuals are considered change agents. However, change agency differs significantly whether one operates from the insider or outsider perspective.

The Insider Change Agent

The insider change agent is aware of biases in him/her and/or in others and is willing to take action when she/he encounters inappropriate words, behaviors or structures.

To communicate the value of diversity, the change agent needs to be supported and encouraged within and by the organization. Others will see that this behavior is rewarded with praise, recognition, etc., and will be more likely to behave similarly.

Typical Behavior

The insider change agent may:

- Leverage her/his credibility with the insider group to promote change
- Tactfully communicate that a discriminatory joke or comment is inappropriate and should not be made in the work environment
- Encourage others to accept colleagues who are different and point out the value that these colleagues bring
- Raise issues about discriminatory and exclusionary behaviors and practices
- Challenge in a non-confrontational manner the *status quo* where appropriate
- Act as a role model
- Mentor outsiders and insiders to effect change in behavior and organizational climate

The Effects

- *For that individual*: The individual has to constantly negotiate her/his role within the insider group. She/he derives personal and professional satisfaction from the investment of personal energy, attention and time to creating a more accepting, accommodating and productive work environment

- *For the workplace*: The change agent is the catalyst for positive changes in the work environment and the mindsets and attitudes of colleagues. An initial period of change and upheaval will give way to a more inclusive workplace. People in the workplace environment become more comfortable as the inclusiveness supports a better atmosphere and more productive work environment. Business performance, creativity, innovation and relationships improve

- *For the organization*: The organization reaps the benefits of diversity, as *outsiders* are encouraged to contribute to their fullest potential. The organization attracts and is able to retain diverse talent and better respond to culturally diverse customers. Diversity and Inclusion become embedded in the organization as distinct cultural assets

Reflections

Who in your environment might act/react as an insider change agent? Based on what observation? What are the effects?

How do you act/react as an insider change agent? Towards which issues and in what situations? What are the effects?

The Outsider Change Agent

The outsider change agent is aware of biases in her/himself and others and is willing to take action when she/he encounters inappropriate words, behaviors or structures. Unlike the insider change agent, the outsider change agent must establish credibility within both the insider and outsider groups in order to create change.

In order to communicate to your employees the value of diversity, it is important that the change agent is supported and encouraged within the organization. Others will see that this behavior is rewarded with praise, recognition, etc., and will try to follow it as well.

Typical Behavior

The outsider change agent may:

- Behave in ways that establish credibility with the insider group
- Tactfully communicate that a discriminatory joke or comment is inappropriate and should not be made in the work environment
- Encourage others to accept colleagues who are different and point out the value that these colleagues bring
- Raise issues about discriminatory and exclusionary behaviors and practices
- Educate others about differences
- Challenge in a non-confrontational manner the *status quo* where appropriate
- Act as a role model and encourage others to act similarly
- Mentor outsiders and insiders to effect change in behavior and organizational climate

The Effects

- _For that individual_: The individual has to constantly negotiate her/his role within both the outsider and insider group. She/he derives personal and professional satisfaction from the investment of personal energy, attention and time to creating a more accepting, accommodating and productive work environment

- *For the workplace*: The change agent is the catalyst for positive changes in the work environment and the mindsets and attitudes of colleagues. An initial period of change and upheaval will give way to a more inclusive workplace. People in the workplace environment become more comfortable as the inclusiveness supports a better atmosphere and more productive work environment. Business performance, creativity, innovation and relationships improve

- *For the organization*: The organization reaps the benefits of diversity as *outsiders* are encouraged to contribute to their fullest potential. The organization attracts and is able to retain diverse talent and respond better to culturally diverse customers. Diversity and Inclusion become embedded in the organization as distinct cultural assets

Reflections

Who in your environment might act/react as an outsider change agent? Based on what observation? What are the effects?

How do you act/react as an outsider change agent? Towards which issues and in what situations? What are the effects?

QUICK REFERENCE:

Insider/Outsider Reactions and Their Consequences

Insider Reactions	Description	Consequences for the Organization
The Unintentional Offender	The individual/group excludes people in the organization because of their differences without being aware of it.	Outsiders feel excluded and isolated from the dominant group.
The Avoider	The individual/group is aware of biases in themselves/others, but is reluctant to address the inappropriate words and behaviors of others.	The organization fails to capitalize on the unique value that diversity brings, as *status quo* is maintained.
The Intentional Offender	The individual/group is aware of behavior and prejudices, but nevertheless continues to exclude outsiders.	A hostile atmosphere is created as outsiders feel they are actively being excluded.
The Change Agent	The individual/group is aware of biases in themselves and others and is willing to take action when they encounter inappropriate words, behaviors or structures.	The organization reaps the benefits of diversity as outsiders are encouraged to contribute to their fullest potential.

I n s i d e r s

Outsider Reactions	Description	Consequences for the Organization
The Assimilator	The individual/group acquiesces to the dominant group – adopts dominant culture and loses all "different" characteristics.	The value of differences is lost - the organization has created a "clone." Potential change and innovation are limited.
The Separatist	The individual/group limits contact with the dominant group, keeping to themselves.	Employees waste time on unnecessary activities designed solely to remove them from the environment in which they feel uncomfortable; absenteeism and high turnover are possible outcomes.
The Fighter	The individual/group actively resists assimilation in an aggressive manner. It is assumed that attack is the best form of defense.	Hostile atmosphere is created by the fighters as they resist assimilation. Often this serves only to reinforce stereotypes. The cause of the problem is hidden and only the result is evident.
The Change Agent	The individual/group works to implement practices and behaviors that are more inclusive of outsiders.	A more inclusive environment is created and outsiders feel encouraged to contribute to the organization.

Outsiders

Change Exclusion Behaviors Through Feedback And/Or Coaching

The inclusive leader holds significant power to reduce the barriers created by passive reinforcers and active perpetuators as well as reinforce the positive momentum brought about by change agents. In fact, it is the manager/leader that needs to act as a change agent in her/his sphere of influence. The most important tools are feedback and coaching.

A critical success factor in using feedback and coaching effectively is to understand and appropriately address the underlying emotional needs and drivers of behavior. The following provide specific recommendations for providing feedback and coaching to each reaction type.

When coaching an _Assimilator_, you will need to:

- Focus on the central need of assimilators to be accepted and fit in with the insider group. Often, a central driver is fear of rejection, negative stereotyping and/or ridicule

- Carefully observe individuals to determine whether they truly are assimilators or not. Since assimilators are hard to distinguish from true insiders, it is difficult to make this determination. Sympathetic probing and observation will help make this assessment

- Communicate frequently and consistently that the organization values differences and that diversity benefits all levels of organizational performance. This is particularly important as the assimilator needs to trust and be convinced that revealing her/his differences will not have a negative affect

    - Provide examples of ways in which the organization benefits from diversity (e.g. bilingual employees can respond to a more diverse customer base)

    - Demonstrate publicly the value placed on diverse experiences, viewpoints, backgrounds and perspectives

- Disclose aspects of your own difference and explain the fears and concerns you have had concerning the related attributes

- Respect personal boundaries and sensitivities individuals may have concerning their hidden "outsider" attributes

When coaching a _Separatist_, you will need to:

- Focus on the need of separatist to be recognized for their unique contributions and value to the insider group. Often, a central driver is the recognition, admiration and valuing of the separatist's unique attributes

- Validate the uniqueness of the individual/group

- Educate the individual about the consequences of setting themselves apart and the value of an inclusive workplace culture

- Coach the employee or group on how to be a part of the larger organization and, at the same time, retain her/his own unique individuality

- Dispel the fear of identity loss that drives separatist behavior

- Enable the employee to be comfortable with her/his differences in a broader context by:

  - Encouraging him/her to confront the challenge and utilize the benefits of being different
  - Linking him/her to change agents in the organization
  - Raising awareness in the employee's work environment about the value of diversity to make it easier for the separatist employee to be part of the organization

- Continuously support the employee throughout the entire process of this challenge

When coaching an _Avoider_, you will need to:

- Focus on the central need of avoiders to reduce social risks by contradicting the dominant insider position and perspective. Safety and risk-avoidance are key drivers of avoider behavior

- Initiate a conversation in which you educate the avoider about the effects of inaction

- Validate the avoider's sense that the behaviors she/he observes are inappropriate

- Cultivate a willingness to change and become a more proactive voice in the organization (provide a sense of safety)

- Empower the person to implement the change in both her/his behavior and environment by:

  - Sending a strong message that inequitable, unfair and/or discriminatory behaviors are not tolerated

  - Rewarding the employee for "proactive behavior"

- Coaching the employee by using specific dilemmas and examples

When coaching an <u>Unintentional Offender</u>, you will need to:

- Focus on the central need of unintentional offenders to be affirmed for her/his positive intentions. Often, a central driver is affirming and reinforcing her/his own "insider-ness"

- Initiate a conversation that will first and foremost raise awareness and educate your employee about the effects of her/his behavior in order to create empathy

- Explain to your employee how being more inclusive will benefit the team and the organization overall

- Recommend specific behaviors or practices such as:

  - Reflecting on her/his use of language

  - Understanding different frames of reference

- Asking open-ended questions

- Being careful with humor in the workplace

- Coach and mentor the employee in the specific area that needs improvement

When coaching an Intentional Offender, you will need to:

- Focus on the central need of the intentional offender to protect her/his power position in the insider group and maintain the *status quo*. Often, a central driver is fear of ambiguity and unpredictable change, as well as losing control

- Determine whether the behaviors and comments are legal issues or go against corporate policy. If so, you must:

    - Clearly outline the legal and/or corporate policy violations of her/his behavior

    - In more severe situations, note the behavior in her/his personnel file

- Initiate a conversation in which you can educate the offender about the effects of her/his behavior on the organizational environment and the company's performance

- Support your employee's efforts and commitment to change by mentoring and coaching her/him

When coaching a Fighter, you will need to:

- Focus on the central need of fighters to be recognized for initializing change and standing up to the dominant insider group against unfair, inequitable and/or unproductive cultural patterns. Often, a central driver is the need to be validated by the outsider group and acknowledged by the insider group

- Educate the employee about the importance of a supportive and open work environment

- Build awareness of the detrimental effects of fighter behavior

- Clearly set the boundaries, limits and expectations of acceptable behavior in the workplace

- Reinforce the importance of valuing diversity, but recommend improved practices such as:

    - Approaching the "offenders" in a polite manner

    - Understanding different frames of reference

    - Explaining differences in a way that educates rather than accuses

    - Assuming positive intent and the positive changeability of people when dealt with properly

- Sensitize the fighter to her/his colleagues' possible lack of awareness of the value of differences

- Provide significant coaching and training in *Constructive Conversations*

When coaching an <u>Insider Change Agent</u>, you will need to:

- Focus on the central need of the insider change agent to transform the *status quo* without jeopardizing her/his insider status

- Recognize and genuinely and sincerely praise the change agent

- Appreciate and reinforce the change agent by:

    - Supporting her/his efforts to change discriminatory behaviors and practices

    - Pointing out the positive effects of her/his behavior on the work environment

    - Recognizing the individual as a role model for insider behavior

- Be a resource for your employee when she/he is trying to solve dilemmas in this area

- Mentor your employee to deal with discrimination in the best way possible

- Encourage others to become change agents
- Leverage the energy, motivation and successes of the change agent throughout the organization

When coaching an <u>Outsider Change Agent</u>, you will need to:

- Focus on the central need of outsider change agents to transform the *status quo* without jeopardizing her/his outsider status
- Support the change agent without compromising her/his credibility with the insider and outsider groups
- Appreciate and reinforce the change agent by:
  - Recognizing her/his efforts in public
  - Supporting her/his efforts to change discriminatory behaviors and practices
  - Pointing out the positive effects of her/his behavior on the work environment
  - Recognizing the individual as a role model
- Be a resource for your employee when she/he is trying to solve dilemmas in this area
- Encourage others to become change agents
- Involve the change agent in teaching and learning about differences
- Leverage the energy, motivation and successes of the change agent throughout the organization

Practice Scenarios

For the scenarios below, identify:

> **a. how the insider-outsider dynamic applies**
>
> **b. the associated risks and/or opportunities**
>
> **c. how feedback or coaching should be applied**

1. Why not Mary?

You are told by your subordinate who is the Team Lead for a global project that he chose Alan to be the subject matter expert for an important and prestigious global project. There was one other qualified candidate, Mary. You ask your Team Leader why she was not chosen. The reply was that the work would involve a lot of travel. Mary is married and may plan to have children; he does not think she is suitable. You happen to know that Alan is a single father who shares childcare responsibilities with his ex-wife.

2. Won't you retire soon?

Ellen was getting increasingly frustrated and discouraged. With 57 years of age and over 24 years of service she has enough experience to see the writing on the wall: As an older employee, she was not welcome anymore. She reports into a team leader almost 20 years younger in a different location. Increasingly, she has been assigned "easy" and "peripheral" assignments and is left out of the loop. Although she has a lot of experience with the customers and the core processes, her implicit knowledge is not sought.

Ellen decided to voice her feelings with her manager. She made a strong case identifying how her knowledge and experience could be leveraged better and adds value to the project. Her manager acted surprised: "Honestly, why would you want to do all this? Won't you retire soon? If we rely too much on you, we will be disadvantaged in the long run. Also, this is a very fast changing project and we have to be on the ball and quick in our responsiveness."

3. What is the matter with Charles?

Charles, a new colleague does not seem to be very friendly to you. In fact, on occasion you sense a degree of hostility. When you enter the office and see him already working in his cubicle, he ignores your greeting. Sometimes, when you ask him a direct question, he does not even answer and continues as if nothing happened. In team meetings, the situation is not any different. Sometimes he responds, and sometimes he doesn't. Your colleagues are equally disturbed and upset, including your manager. Most have reduced their contact with him to a minimum. Even Sarah, your manager, is frustrated and gives him assignments that do not involve a lot of team contact.

Yesterday, you mentioned this to an old friend and colleague from a different department who had worked with Charles in his previous job. Your friend was very surprised at your negative reaction to Charles. "Didn't he tell you?," he exclaimed, "Charles has always had a hearing disability!"

4. He is just tired!

Paul has worked at the same large, prestigious corporation for the past 15 years and is appreciated and well liked by everyone in his department. He is outgoing and has a warm personality and a great sense of humor. However, his colleagues are completely unaware of the turmoil he often feels. Paul is gay and has not dared to come out to his co-workers. His male and female colleagues have often made derogatory remarks and joked about gays and lesbians, particularly with the recent debate about gay marriage.

He is hurt by their attitudes. He fears the judgment and potential repercussions of revealing his sexual orientation, though it is something he has wanted to do for a long time. Of course, Paul's sexual orientation has nothing to do with his work, but it is an integral part of his identity; something he does not want to be ashamed of any longer. When others talk about their families or personal problems, he has never been able to share in the discussion. He often deflects the situation with humor. Paul is just tired - tired of hiding, denying and the frustration that has mounted over the years. At some point soon, he is going to have to come out.

5. What do you think?

Thomas was looking forward to meeting the new member of the team. He had heard a lot about Kara and seen her name on email copy and distribution lists, but they had never met in person. He always felt that this all male team needed a woman. It was fortunate that the annual team meeting was scheduled so soon after Kara joined. This would surely facilitate working together.

At the meeting, Thomas was surprised that his team members did not seem to share his enthusiasm. None of them extended themselves to her, and he noticed a few unkind comments. Over drinks at the bar with a few of them, George seemed to speak for the majority when he leaned over and asked: "Tom, what do you think of our new "diversity colleague"? I guess we fulfilled the quota all in one – a woman and she's black! Just to keep the political correctness police off our back!"

6. Tapping New Markets

You are charged with opening new local markets to foster growth and innovation. Traditional markets are highly saturated; however, the 72% of households that are part of the emergence and subsistence market are virtually untapped. You strongly suspect a viable and profitable opportunity, however:

- Most of your team members disagree and see little, if any potential

- Your marketing group has very little insight into this market sector and does not think the advertisement expenditure worthwhile

- Your sales organisation claims that the margins would not support the new sales and distribution networks that are necessary

- Management maintains that the compliance requirement with U.S. manufacturing standards creates a cost structure that cannot compete with the multitude of low-cost, small scale operations that traditionally cater to that market

7. A Matter of Style

Everyone in the office loves Thandiwe. She is an effective and skilled manager who likes to use her distinctive "human touch" to relate to her employees and colleagues. Her friendly and outgoing nature has made her a number of friends even among senior management. Her motivation and drive together with her intelligence and capabilities have clearly made her a high potential employee, and she has been recommended for participation in the company's multi-year *Leadership Development Program (LDP)*.

Very recently, Thandiwe's popularity and bright perspective has been shattered. For unspecified reasons, her manager was suddenly transferred to another division. His replacement, Mr. van der Zander has not warmed up to her at all.

She is not the only one affected by his abrasive, directive, blunt, dry and results-focused work and management style, but she took the impact of this drastic change particularly hard. Thandiwe's previous manager encouraged harmony and collaboration, and she was specifically attuned to the work-life balance issues in the workplace. Geert van der Zander, by contrast, provides detailed directions and expects single-minded execution. He gets irritated and angry at what he calls "chit chat" and frequently remarks: "We are not a social club here! This is a *work*place!"

Thandiwe was very upset and embarrassed. Mr. van der Zander chastised her in front of her colleagues for not having been in the office for what he called "*critical meetings and planning discussions.*" Flexibility is a particular concern to her since she needs to care for both her 3 year old and her ailing mother of 76.

Thandiwe has tried a few times to discuss their different styles and expectations with Mr. van der Zander but he has been unreceptive. The last time he simply said: "*Look, this group has not been doing as well as it should. That's why I am here now. If everyone would just focus on their work, we would all be better off; including you.*"

She left his office discouraged and angry. The mood at work had clearly changed and the fun and excitement were gone. Even her colleagues seem more distant. She was wondering why she had not heard more about the Leadership Development Program. She was wondering whether it was time to look for a different employer.

8. He just doesn't fit!

One of your colleagues validated your suspicion when she let you know that she overheard one of your managers, Mishail, mention that he decided against promoting Markus into a different department. Mishail supposedly did not support Markus's candidacy because of his age (late 40s). He said that Markus would have a hard time fitting in with the youth culture he has been cultivating in that organization.

■ Engage in Constructive Conversations

Anyone experiencing exclusion situations, particularly change agents, require a safe way to discuss their experiences, and surface and address the root causes of insider-outsider dynamics. Because the associated issues and challenges tend to be complex, personal and emotional; a specific skill is required to avoid inadvertently aggravating the situation. We call this skill *Constructive Conversations*. This approach synthesizes both research and practical experience[4].

Constructive Conversations serve to establish and agree on resolutions, practices and processes that are more acceptable and inclusive. Learning how to engage in constructive conversations, therefore, helps managers, employees, and their organization to appropriately address and prevent unconstructive situations and interactions.

There are two types of Constructive Conversations:

> **Proactive** – these are conversations conducted when no immediate critical issue exists. The objective is to explore Frames of Reference to foster mutual understanding. It is best applied to:

- establish rapport
- overcome discomfort based on perceived differences
- create open communication

> **Reactive** – these are conversations conducted when a critical issue exists. The objective is to address the issue constructively, reduce conflict and establish commitment to positive resolutions. It is best applied to:

- diffuse tension
- create clarity and common ground
- gain commitment to act

While the Constructive Conversation approach is based on five distinct phases, only the first three are required in proactive conversations. All five are required to address critical issues.

Constructive Conversations

It may be helpful to understand constructive conversations as a specific sequence of five distinct, yet inter-related, phases. The length of each phase will vary by issue, individuals, and the overall cultural backgrounds and contexts involved. In some situations, the entire five phases can be captured in a few minutes, in others; each phase may required an in-depth and lengthy exchange.

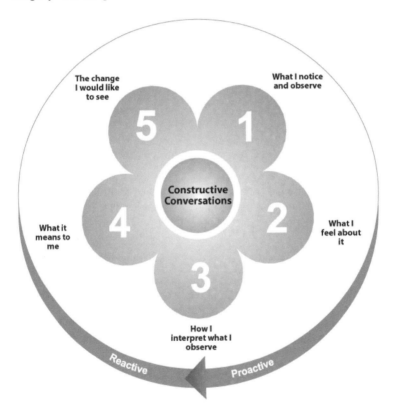

Illustration 4.2: Constructive Conversations

Illustration 4.2 above captures this idea and articulates the main issues and topics upon which each particular phase should center.

Before exploring each phase individually, it is useful to understand the recommended phasing of this approach. This is particularly important, as it runs counter to the way managers and leaders typically approach these type of conversations.

The recommended approach synthesized both research and practical experience[4]. These approaches differentiate distinct levels of experience:

- The *issue level*; i.e., what occurs

- The *emotional level*; i.e., how you feel about the issue/situation

- The *Frame of Reference level*; i.e., how we perceive, evaluate and relate to what occurs

- The *identity/needs level*; i.e., what the issue means to us and which needs are associated with it

It is recommended that for conversations to be constructive and lead to positive resolutions and behavioral change, all four levels should be included and addressed.

With this in mind, we recommend applying a specific structure to conversations about exclusion/inclusion topics and related social and personal experiences.

Start by stating your **observations** in a non-judgmental way, particularly avoiding negative inferences and assumptions. While this sounds easy, it is actually very difficult in practice. It is, however, a critical foundation to open up the conversation and avoid closing it down because our judgments and inferences have caused defensiveness in our counterpart(s).

Once the observation and experiences are described in this fashion, another difficult task needs to be mastered, namely to articulate your **emotions** associated with the situation or condition you are describing. This may be a counterintuitive recommendation, but it increases your likelihood of connecting with your counterpart(s) through empathy. Acknowledging and describing the emotional effects early in the conversation grounds the subsequent exploration of the different interpretation of behaviors and experiences in our common human bond.

On the basis of empathy and a revelation of the emotions connected to a particular situation, the groundwork exists for an explanation and exploration of the *interpretations* that are involved. This is an important step as our interpretations are reflections of our Frame of Reference. We often uncover hidden and highly significant differences in perceptions, expectations and evaluations that motivate behaviors and reactions. These can often reflect differing cultural orientations as well.

We have thus identified the root connections with which we make sense of our experiences and established shared understanding. We have not yet put them in the social context of the specific roles and relationships involved. To do so, we need to disclose the deeper and personal *meaning* of the situation and the connected needs.

Once revealed and shared, we can now request the specific *change we would like to see*. Having created empathy as the foundation for this conversation, we have appropriately contextualized our request and created the conditions for a constructive resolution.

However, success with Constructive Conversations also depends on one's ability to (a) assume positive intent, (b) listen and observe non-judgmentally, and (c) reflect honestly on the intentions and needs involved. On the following pages we will provide suggestions for applying Constructive Conversations section-by-section and illustrate their use.

Phase 1:
What I notice and observe

Your goal in this phase is to open up the conversation in as positive and constructive a way as possible. This lays the foundation for the rest of the conversation. Since you are using this approach to bring up critical and difficult personal and interpersonal issues, your main objective should be to avoid closing down your counterpart because your judgments and inferences trigger defensiveness on her/his part.

Creating willingness to engage involves the *non-judgmental* description of what you are noticing and observing; i.e., of how the situation(s) concerned are manifested.

Keys to success:

- Describe your observations without judgments and evaluations
- Avoid negative inferences or assumptions

Exercise:

It is rather difficult to describe a situation in a truly non-judgmental way, avoiding negative inferences or assumptions. Review the following sentences and identify which ones are truly observations and which ones are actually judgements.

A. He was angry without reason

B. She was tapping her fingers during the meeting

C. You work too much

D. She did not consult me on this issue

E. I am excluded from all important decisions

F. You always complain and do not take action

NOTE: see page 94 for the solutions

Exercise:

Choose any relevant situation and describe it in non-judgmental terms, without negative inferences and assumptions.

Example: In a group, ask someone to sit in a slumping position, yawn, and look around the room without focusing on the speaker. Then ask others what they see. Often, those observing this behavior would say they "observed" the person being tired, or uninterested and bored. In actuality, the only observation is that the person is slumping in the chair, yawning and looking around the room. The other descriptions are judgements rather than observations.

Phase 2:
What I feel about it

Once you have created willingness to engage with your counterpart, your focus should be directed on maintaining the contact and creating openness with each other. Doing so is best accomplished by articulating your emotions connected with the situation or condition you have described. Although sometimes difficult and counterintuitive to many workplaces, you nevertheless increase your likelihood of connecting with your counterpart(s) through empathy. Acknowledging and describing your emotional reactions early in the conversation grounds the subsequent exploration of the different interpretation of behaviors and experiences in a common human bond.

It is important to note that these first two phases of the model are not arguable by the other person. We have described *our* observations and shared *our* feelings without evaluations or interpretations that must be defended or can be perceived as an attack on the other person.

Keys to success:
- State your personal feelings
- Avoid blame
- Take responsibility for your emotions
- Do not interpret your emotions

Although emotions are often considered inappropriate in a work environment, remember that you are *discussing,* not demonstrating them. Be aware of confusing a statement of feeling with the interpretation of feelings. Common language use often makes it difficult to truly be in touch with what we feel and injects the words we use with assumptions about another's intent and motivation.

Exercise

Consider the following lists of words. Notice that interpretations require another person in the situation while feelings are only within an individual.

Interpretations: abandoned, betrayed, cheated, bullied, diminished, intimidated, manipulated, overworked, pressured, provoked, put down, rejected, unseen, unsupported

Feelings: afraid, aggravated, embarrassed, lonely, mad, resentful, disturbed, nervous, sad, amused, confident, delighted, thankful, fulfilled, glad, inspired

Exercise

Which of the expressions below are really interpretations vs. feelings?

A. I feel frustrated   **D. I feel misunderstood**
B. I feel ignored   **E. I feel annoyed**
C. I feel attacked   **F. I feel pressured**

NOTE: see page 94 for the solutions

**Phase 3:
How I interpret
what I observe**

The previous phase should have laid the important groundwork of empathy and connection upon which we can now build. In Phase 3 we explain and explore how to interpret what we have previously noticed and observed. Here, we use our awareness of our own Frame of Reference and its origins. In sharing and comparing our interpretations with a counterpart, we uncover hidden and highly significant differences in the perceptions, expectations and evaluations that motivate behaviors and reactions.

Keys to success

- Be aware of your own *Frame of Reference* and its origins
- Be open and acknowledge the validity of other interpretations
- Focus on how *you* make sense of what is happening
- Avoid absolute statements (e.g., this is …)

You will notice that many of the sensitive and difficult issues addressed in this fashion have their root cause in differing interpretations due to various *Frames of Reference* of the individuals involved. Of course the degree with which we are aware of our own Frame of Reference is a critical element for the success of this phase.

Phase 4:
What it means to me

By this point, we have identified key differences. However, we have not yet put them in the social context of the specific needs, roles and relationships involved. To do so, we need to disclose the deeper and personal meaning of the situation and the connected needs. For example, a team member may articulate that she/he wants to be a valuable contributor to the team and feels that a given situation is preventing this from happening. An employee may reveal her/his desire to be considered respectful or loyal; a manager may want to be fair in a given situation.

Keys to success

- Articulate *why* this is important to *you*
- Identify how the situation connects to your needs
- Connect your interpretation to the significance of the situation
- Be honest about your motivation and intent

Be aware that when reflecting on the meaning and significance of a particular issue that there is rarely one single, simple meaning. Honest reflection is like peeling an onion.

For example, if an employee asks to be reassigned to another team, there are often many needs beyond the stated reason for the request. The employee may identify the reason as the need for advancement. The employee may also be uncomfortable with the style of the team leader, find the work tedious, or believe the project will be unsuccessful. While it is not necessary to reveal publicly all the reasons, it is important to understand them for self awareness.

It is seldom a simple, single meaning!

Illustration 4.3: Constructive Conversations

Reflection

Think about the last conflict situation you were in (either personal or work related). What was important to you and why? How was your behavior and interpretation connected to your frame of reference in the situation?

Phase 5:
The change I would like to see

We have appropriately contextualized our request and created the conditions for a constructive resolution. In the final phase, we make a request for specific changes.

Keys to success:
- Be as specific about your request as possible
- Adopt the SMART criteria for your request

> **S** pecific
> **M** easurable
> **A** ttainable
> **R** ealistic
> **T** rackable/Timebound

- Be clear that a request is NOT a demand

The last point is very important. Constructive Conversations, by their very nature, are best applied in situations in which it would be counterproductive to demand or communicate in a demanding/commanding style.

The difference between a request and a demand is that with a demand others believe they will be blamed or punished if they do not comply. A request presents the opportunity for the other to be involved in the outcome which increases the potential for a satisfactory resolution. For example, if you make a demand there are only two choices of action for the other, submission or rebellion. In a highly charged situation, you are likely to meet resistance with a demand. This can easily undermine the entire positive foundation you have created through the previous steps.

Exercise

Think about a change you would like to see in your personal or business context. State this change as a SMART request.

Practice Scenarios

For the following scenarios, identify:

> **a. how Constructive Conversation can be productively applied**
>
> **b. who should initiate the conversation**
>
> **c. how a Constructive Conversation is best initiated**

1. Mei Yen's Frustration

Mei Yen is an integral part of a geographically dispersed team. As a field representative, she needs to coordinate her activities closely with her steering committee consisting of five individuals (Tokito, Celia, Suzanna, Phillipe, and Sean, the team leader). The entire steering committee is located at the regional headquarters.

Every two weeks, she takes part in a team conference call. Since the steering committee members are located at the same site, they get together in a conference room with various field representatives calling in over the speaker phone.

Mei does not look forward to these calls. Typically, she spends the beginning of each call listening to the four other's small talk. Their sporadic laughter, jokes and allusions alienate her from the conversations as she cannot see them interact. Mei cannot fully explain all her issues and concerns and feels distant from her team members. She attributes some of this to her accent and discomfort with colloquial use of English. In addition, she is the only one not using English on a daily basis.

Mei's frustration has been growing over the past months. She feels increasingly disrespected and undervalued. And when she found out that the team made decisions ignoring her input about the local cultural conditions, she was absolutely furious.

2. She can sense it!

For several months now, Sarah Farouq has been feeling increasingly alienated at work. More and more often these days, her colleagues fall silent when she passes by. Sometimes, it is as if she could hear their thoughts.

People see her headscarf and immediately a chain of associations is set in motion: headscarf, Muslim, Arab, potential terrorist. She senses it. People have been distant, more suspicious and distrusting of Sarah. Colleagues who used to exchange small talk with her have not done so in weeks.

Sarah is upset at this palpable change in the environment around her. Her clothing has become as much a liability as her thick foreign accent. When she was re-assigned to a project that required her to work more "independently" rather than in a team, her sadness turned into plain anger. To her, this "independence" meant isolation and amounted to a punishment. With such treatment, she will not stay long with the organization.

3. The Forecasting Dilemma

Below are two perspectives on the same situation

A. A colleague in a headquarters function tells you about the following frustration:

> *"It is absolutely predictable: I simply cannot get certain regions to comply with my reporting requirements. I get so frustrated when I find that they are not as responsive and committed as we strive to be. I sent out the reporting requirements in advance a while ago. I followed up with an e-mail indicating the deadline and precise reporting format; and I get no reply or just resistance. I am so frustrated – some seem to not even understand why and how the forecasting process operates - as if they would not benefit from it. In my headquarters function I often wonder why the others do not operate with the same kind of urgency and perspective that we have. It's so predictable. I never get the reports in on time, even when I try to provide a more aggressive due date and put more pressure."*

B. A colleague from a regional office tells you about the same situation:

"I get so annoyed at these messages from headquarters marked as 'urgent', especially the most recent one concerning forecasting! –Forecasting? ... Under our conditions, with this persistent economic and political instability, how can I provide anything that can possibly be reasonable or realistic?

And then, whatever I provide, I will be held responsible for in the end. This can make my group look bad in some regional meeting where nobody understands our business conditions here anyway. So what is the value?

In addition, most of the information they want they already have. I provided it to them before. Of course, not in the format they want it in, but that is for their convenience only. Why do I have to put everything into their format if the information is not really useful for me anyway? And this is not even my job! I am in a customer facing role and in an already difficult economic climate. That's what I need to focus on – if I don't, there really will be nothing to forecast. I have stopped taking these 'urgent emails' seriously and sometimes I respond, only much later."

4. I don't fit the profile!

You have noticed that your manager seems to rely heavily on another colleague. When confronted with particularly challenging issues and situations, your manager tends to seek input from your colleague, ignoring you. Your colleague also seems to be entrusted with more difficult and high-visibility assignments and often is selected to attend high profile client events. Although you have a very different approach and work style, you have a clear track record on comparable challenges with past jobs. Your achievements and skills just don't seem to be recognized by this manager.

Constructive Conversation Preparation Exercise

Identify a personal situation in which a Constructive Conversation could enable you to bring about greater inclusion in your sphere of influence. Use the Worksheet below to prepare.

	What you might say	Your Notes
Phase 1: What I notice and observe • Describe non-judgmentally • Avoid negative inferences or assumptions	I see I notice I observe	
Phase 2: What I feel about it • State your feelings • Avoid blame • Take responsibility for your feelings	I feel … when … I react with … I get very …	
Phase 3: How I interpret what I observe • State how you interpret the situation • Avoid absolute statements	I interpret this as … To me this means … Based on my experience …	
Phase 4: What it means to me • Focus on the significance of the situation for you • Articulate why it is important to you	I would like to be … I do not want … It is important to me that …	

Phase 5: The change I would like to see • Request SMART actions • Be aware that a request is NOT a demand	*S* pecific *M* easurable *A* ttainable *R* ealistic *T* rackable / Time-bound	

Exercise Solutions

Page 82:
Only sentence B is an observation. All others contain hidden judgments.

Depending on the interpretation of "consult", question D can also be considered an interpretation. For example, does "consult" mean ask once or a prolonged involvement?

Page 84:
Sentences, A, B, C, and D, and contain interpretations that would better be stated as such. Only E is a feeling. However, F can be either a feeling or an interpretation. If the pressure is perceived as coming from someone else, it is an interpretation. If from the pressure is coming from within, it is a feeling.

Chapter 5

STEP 3: Embed Inclusion Practices into the Culture

Constructive Conversations are important to initiate change, but alone are clearly insufficient to sustain it. To accomplish this, the established resolutions, practices and processes need to become institutionalized within the leader's sphere of influence. Here the leader needs to conscientiously apply her/his power to transmit, embed and/or change the organization's culture. This power resides in:

- What she/he pays attention to, measures and controls

- Her/his reactions to critical incidents and crises

- What she/he teaches and coaches

- What example she/he sets and which behaviors she/he models

- What she/he informally reinforces and rewards

- How she/he formally allocates rewards and recognition

- Criteria she/he uses to recruit, select, engage and promote employees, partners, contractors and/or suppliers

Ideally, the individual leader will apply her/his levers within the framework of a diversity and inclusion initiative and/or change strategy for the organization culture. Most inclusion initiatives however, will require a number of specific actions and practices focused on the relevance of inclusion on three key domains actualized by individual effectiveness:

Competitiveness in the Marketplace

♦ Link to client and customer patterns, trends, expectations, needs, etc.

Organizational Capability

♦ Relevant talent management, high levels of employee motivation satisfaction and commitment, conducive organizational culture and climate, etc.

Team Effectiveness and Collaboration

♦ Effective work groups, business unit, cross-functional collaboration, global teams, sourcing and out-sourcing relationships, etc.

Exploration Exercise:

Review the list of potential actions below and mark those that you can champion or adopt in your sphere of influence.

This list is not complete. Consider additional actions that are relevant and meaningful in your context and add them to the list.

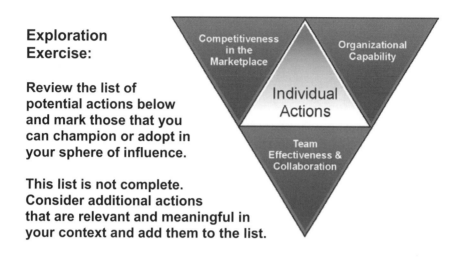

1. **Competitiveness in the Marketplace**

☐ Evaluate trends in society and in the marketplace and assess their relevance and importance for your business/organization

☐ Track developments in the market and with your customers and clients carefully; discuss and explore changes, trends and opportunities with them

☐ Extrapolate demographic trends of utilization and consumption in your industry; assess your strategy and tactics accordingly

☐ Assess the relevance of diversity and inclusion to your business strategy and tactics

☐ Challenge underlying assumptions about markets, clients, customers and partners

☐ When designing, developing and communicating products for the global market, leverage the multiple viewpoints of all stakeholders by ensuring appropriate communication and creative processes

☐ Ensure that you design, develop and market global products in a culturally competent way

☐ When partnering and collaborating across organizations, map out the hidden differences in expectations, approaches, and business practices

☐ Surface and address differences in organizational culture when pursuing joint ventures, mergers or acquisitions

☐ Build the requisite diversity and cultural competence of your sales, marketing and delivery force when working with clients worldwide

☐ Build the requisite diversity and cultural competence of those that manage vendor/supplier or partner relationships

☐ Evaluate your organization's culture and surface embedded "cultural risk factors" vis-à-vis the requirements of the market

☐ Practice Constructive Conversations to address issues in client, supplier and partner relations

☐ Take steps to proactively reduce the cultural risk factors in your client/customer and supplier relationship

☐ Other (please specify):

2. Organizational Capability

☐ Ensure that the expectations, risks and opportunities connected to inclusion, diversity and cultural competence are relevant and credibly communicated

☐ Identify specific barriers to inclusiveness and explore how insider-outsider dynamics apply in your sphere of influence though conversations and/or focus groups

☐ Involve all individuals in removing barriers

☐ Foster an organizational culture that is attractive to a broad range of employees

☐ Ensure recruitment is based on selecting from as diverse a talent pool as possible

☐ Ensure that the broadest range of perspectives are applied to problem solving

☐ Clearly articulate the behavioral expectations and cultural standards in your sphere of influence

☐ Cultivate a climate of trust, tolerance and openness for differences

☐ Analyze compensation of employees and ensure fair and equitable remuneration

☐ Track and discuss employee satisfaction and commitment particularly concerning diversity and inclusiveness issues

☐ Establish and reinforce guiding principles that enable inclusiveness in information sharing, decision making, meetings, use of communication tools, etc.

☐ Evaluate and enhance the inclusiveness of evaluation, recognition, rewards, and award systems within the organization

☐ Foster "outsiders on the inside" as a key source of organizational adaptability, innovation and creativity

☐ Establish and participate in forums that encourage an open forum for discussion and conflict resolution

☐ Ensure that open and constructive opinions are appropriately acknowledged and acted upon (provide follow up)

☐ Apply Constructive Conversations to address divisions, tensions and conflicts that stem from differences

☐ Institute reward and recognition program and communication programs supporting inclusive leadership

☐ Model the behaviors you want to see (e.g., standards for respect, etc.)

☐ Other (please specify):

3. Team Effectiveness and Collaboration

☐ Ensure that the viewpoints, expectations and perspectives of all stakeholders in the team's success are surfaced and understood

☐ Identify diversity and cultural gaps that may affect the success of the team and identify steps to manage them

☐ Identify barriers to team communication and collaboration and agree on equitable processes (e.g., time zone differences, access to communication technology, resources, etc.)

☐ Do not limit your team selection by too narrow a success or competency profile

☐ Observe colleagues' and team member's behaviors, actions and interactions

☐ Discuss the needs of team members for flexibility and agree on guidelines for work flexibility

☐ Include self- and other-awareness measures in formal and informal team development processes

☐ Encourage the sharing of diverse backgrounds, experiences, perspectives among all team members and colleagues

☐ Develop team and meeting norms (i.e., an inclusive team culture) based on an understanding of differences in personality, functional and professional background, cultural background and languages

☐ Actively monitor and track the inclusiveness of teamwork and collaboration through the use of "cultural/inclusion mentors" (perhaps on a rotational basis)

☐ Apply Constructive Conversations proactively to build rapport and understanding of team members, particularly in the team initialization phase

☐ Use Constructive Conversations reactively to address critical issues, tensions and conflict and establish inclusive resolutions

❑ Develop and practice new member integration processes based on explicit introduction of differences in *Frame of Reference,* experience and culture

❑ Foster continuous learning about relevant diversity and inclusion related topics (e.g., analysis of relevant data, topical briefings, rotate responsibilities for learning about specific issues among team members, etc.)

❑ Ensure that team activities are inclusive and not based on the preference of only a few (Also: check any religious, ethnic or national holidays when scheduling events and understand any eating restrictions)

❑ Other (please specify):

Any of the above needs to be grounded in your **individual** skills and action. Consider how you can apply and/or enhance any of the following:

❑ Observe the insider-outsider interactions in your sphere of influence and identify issues that need to be addressed

❑ Act as a change agent in your sphere of influence (speak out when processes, systems or practices are not inclusive and create undesirable barriers)

❑ Develop awareness of how your *Frame of Reference* contrasts or overlaps with others and affects your sphere of influence (beware of individual or collective blind-spots)

❑ Explore differences with others and identify their benefits and hidden opportunities

❑ Broaden your language and communication style to ensure a broad level of effectiveness (particularly in a global, cross-cultural context)

❑ Explore the *real* cultural environment you create through what you tacitly expect, reinforce and reward through open feedback from others

❑ Reflect on how your own biases and prejudices affect your evaluation of situations, individuals and groups

☐ Ensure that you assign tasks equitably and consider the developmental needs of your employees (avoid cultivating a single "go to person" while not providing others with opportunities to grow)

☐ Provide equal access to information, both formal and informal (avoid contributing to situations in which information creates undesirable insider-outsider divisions)

☐ Give public and private recognition to others for behaving in inclusive ways

☐ Apply constructive conversations in difficult situations with your manager, colleagues, and counterparts

☐ Let others know when their behavior is unacceptable or unproductive for an inclusive culture - this has added weight if the behavioral expectations and organizational values of your organization are set, communicated and reinforced

☐ Other (please specify):

CHAPTER 6

Application Exercises

This section consists of various scenario and application exercises. They cover a wide range of issues to which the skills of Inclusive Leadership can be meaningfully applied. They have been inspired by real situations and were developed specifically to help individuals practice the spectrum of skills introduced in this Guide.

For the given scenario, explore the following questions:

1. How are specific workforce and marketplace challenges related to the scenario?

2. How do differences in *Frame of Reference* affect the given situation?

3. How does the insider-outsider relationship apply to this scenario? What are the inherent risks and opportunities?

4. How could the exclusion situation be transformed?

5. What practices could/should be embedded in the culture as a result? What would it take to sustain these practices?

Scenario 1: The Harion Debacle

You feel a headache coming on from just thinking about the upcoming meeting of your newly formed global, cross-functional team. The team's mission is to improve the market share of *Harion* and identify additional markets and applications. *Harion* had first been heralded as a triumph and scientific breakthrough. However, quality defects during the launch caused a significant setback, of which your competitor was quick to take advantage.

Your leadership is determined to make *Harion* profitable within only 12 months or else cancel *Harion* altogether. The responsibility for making *Harion* viable rests squarely on your team's shoulders. Every time you remember the first team meeting, you are reminded that you, as the project leader, are bearing the brunt of that responsibility. In the first meeting:

- The three representatives from R&D were visibly and vocally upset with the manufacturing group about having "messed up" their hard work. Dr. Hasselmann (who had a vital research role and subsequently published several articles on the breakthrough findings on the project) went even further and blamed manufacturing with "sabotage" and "undermining the scientific value and integrity of the organization." He questioned the value of the R&D contributions to this effort, unless "significant consequences" would ensue for the other functions, particularly manufacturing, and people with proper perspectives, qualifications, and credentials were brought on board."

- Mr. Gregory Jamison, one of the two manufacturing representatives, was just as irritated and underhandedly remarked that "not everyone is privileged to be as intelligent, as free of faults as the 'gentlemen from R&D.'" He then reminded the team that had management not pressured for a relocation of the manufacturing facility to a lower-cost country, the *Harion* debacle could have surely been avoided.

- Mr. Ricard Alstrom, the only representative from Finance, launched a long explanation to justify management's decision to relocate manufacturing facilities and streamline production processes. He outlined the financial and performance implications and subtly remarked: "Frankly, we are a business after all, not a labor union or an institute for pure research."

- Ms. Allison Wong, the one representative from Marketing, remained remarkably quiet during this wrangle. She had tried to interject a few times but was quickly overshadowed by the others and discouraged soon thereafter. You knew she had some interesting ideas about linking Harion to various "lifestyle products." She also had some focus group insights to share.

How should you, who has been with the organization for only eight months now approach this team? How can you make Harion a success story? After all, this is your first high visibility assignment with your new employer.

Scenario 2: Reassigned?

Alexandra did not understand why she was suddenly reassigned to a different account. She had been the only woman on the Jetco team. She had worked on Jetco for the past year and, from her perspective, had built good rapport and relationships with her Jetco counterparts and had achieved all her project milestones on time and within budget.

Alexandra had been thrilled about working on Jetco; everyone knows that it is one of the biggest and most important international clients. The visibility of this strategic project would be important for her resume and career. All this would be gone now with the new assignment to a much smaller and more routine account.

When Alexandra complained about this situation at lunch to colleagues, Susan, an older colleague who she met as a participant in a Leadership Development Program years ago, leaned over and said: "I've heard that your reassignment was due to a request by the client to not have any women on the account team."

Alexandra was furious. Her manager had told her very little about the specific reasons for her reassignment, only that the new account needed her skills and that the Jetco team was overstaffed anyway. Was this a set up?

Scenario 3: Attracting and Retaining Talent

Your organization is having a very difficult time finding qualified talent. The competencies and training you require are complex and highly specific. Competition for the small pool of talent is very high. In addition, the enrollment profile at training institutions and universities is not any more encouraging. The total number of graduates is projected to decline over the next decade, while the enrollment of women in this traditionally male discipline will quadruple.

You get worried when you take a closer look at your organization. First, morale and commitment levels are average. The organizational survey indicates that the comparatively low compensation levels are a cause for widespread dissatisfaction. At the same time, you have been seeing an increased attrition by women. It seems that you are not able to retain women at mid-level management levels or higher.

Exit interviews with this population indicate a general perception of (cultural) unspecified barriers for women; a lack of feeling supported or understood, unrealistic overload and unmanageable expectations.

Putting all this together, you are worried about your organization's future competitiveness.

Scenario 4: Young, Hip, Smart, Fast

Over the past decade, the organization has actively focused on cultivating and projecting a different image to its customers: young, hip, fast, and smart. Recruitment and development have focused on these attributes and they have seeped into many facets of the culture. The organization has adopted an open office space concept and changed its office design standards to an ultra-modern look. In meetings, quick thinking and dazzling, eloquent presentations have become as much part of the success profile, as fashionable clothing and a youthful, dynamic interaction style.

The organization has had a very difficult time recruiting and retaining employees 40 or older and those who tend to have a more reflective and low key style. This is slowly developing into a significant crisis, due to the development and shifting age distribution in the workforce and the commensurate aging of key market segments. The pool of new talent is shrinking, the organization is growing, valuable experience is either leaving or difficult to attract.

Scenario 5: Good intentions are not enough

Ever since the launch of the new advertising campaign, the organization has registered an increase in customer complaints. It certainly appeared that what was supposed to be a radical step in re-branding the company by displaying its awareness of consumer diversity, was about to back-fire. Certain ethnic groups felt stereotyped and misrepresented. They objected to the biases and stereotypes reproduced in the advertisement spots.

These complaints were difficult to reconcile. The team responsible for the advertisement campaign had been careful to model the depiction of the various consumer segments based on results of market research and focus groups.

Scenario 6: Managing Change

The V.P. of your organization presented an overview of recent study results that he felt would significantly improve the just-in-time delivery capability of aftermarket products starting at the production floor. He passionately elaborated on the vision of this project and presented a high-level change plan. Most attendees responded well to the presentation. However, managers from a recent acquisition were not certain that his conclusions and the accompanying implementation timetable were adequate to warrant a decision about piloting a line change.

They vehemently voiced their objections and asked for additional information and data, including: 1) provide greater detail about the basic research and concept testing, 2) indicate what impact the pilot change would have on their department workload, and 3) delineate how various project roles would be distributed among the production line staff to implement the change. Some of the managers were clearly outraged; two key leaders even walked out of the meeting.

Scenario 7: Losing Face

Communication among your global team members, located in Italy, Germany, Mexico, and the U.S. is not working well. Decision making is slow, frustration is mounting and team members are not responsive to each other. Communication technology is a particular source of frustration.

Jop DeBeers, leader of a customer-facing group in the Netherlands, has been complaining bitterly for months about the team's lack of responsiveness. He describes how his team is embarrassed in front of the client, because it relies on the speedy and accurate receipt of information from your team. He laments that urgent e-mail requests remain unanswered, people are inaccessible through voicemail, and time differences make a speedy and efficient response difficult. He is furious and makes no attempts to hide his anger just about every time you talk with him. He constantly points out that most often the wrong information is sent or the information simply arrives too late.

Scenario 8: Leveraging Insight

Your accounts receivable operation is having a very difficult time with customers not following through on their payment promises. The economic difficulties in the region significantly contribute to this situation. An additional complication is the organization culture: hierarchical behavior among the employees, their focus on complying with the prescribed, yet inflexible processes, low levels of motivation and engagement, and strong silos among the business units.

As the new manager of the organization, you are expected to significantly improve organization results. You suspect that both sales and accounts receivable representatives possess valuable insight into the customer operations and motivation which should be leveraged.

Scenario 9A: The 80:20 Fool

Below are two perspectives on the same situation:

<u>You are talking to a colleague who tells you about the following frustration</u>:

> *You know, our manager is so typical! I cannot believe it. We have this aggressive release deadline and we have been so nervous because not all components are thoroughly tested. Some features are not even developed. With only one more week to go, and so much to do, I am not sure how we will get things done. Even if all of us worked through the nights, it is simply impossible to get a high quality solution released.*
>
> *We need more resources and time to do the job right, but he is not concerned at all and wants to release whatever we have. Healways says: "In the context of the on-demand strategy, the 80:20 rule is good enough. We need to get things out fast. When we are 80% there, it's good enough. We can always fix and upgrade later." This is such a typical attitude from our U.S. managers.*
>
> *I simply do not understand this attitude. It seems foolish. And in the same breath they will talk about integrity and respect? Why should I compromise my professional standards and integrity just to be quick!? And, doesn't on-demand mean that the solution is optimally adapted and responsive to the specific needs, requirements and situation of our client? I simply do not understand. What is so great about meeting an unrealistic deadline and creating an unsatisfied client? I tried to talk to him about this many times, but he just gets upset and repeats the 80:20 story.*

Scenario 9B: They Need to Get With The Program

<u>You are talking to a colleague and she/he tells you about the following frustration</u>:

> *You know, they just don't get it! I don't understand why it is so hard for them to understand. We are in the on-demand, just-in-time era and that means change for all of us. But this team of mine is determined to resist change. They constantly point out that we should not release this product because not everything is in place and properly tested. You know, how can we compete in the on-demand world if we do not rigorously apply the 80:20 rule? We need to get things out fast. When we are 80% there, it's good enough. We can always fix and upgrade later. We are 80% there with this product, so we need to release it – that's quick and on-demand.*
>
> *My team does not get it. They talk about professional standards and integrity, but it is really a matter of survival in a very competitive market. Speed and responsiveness are key. This is why we need the right people to win; we cannot afford to hesitate or linger. They either get with the program or they should not be on this team. We need to be aggressive and get things out if we want to dominate the market.*
>
> *Frankly, I think that most of my team simply refuses to understand this. We need to weed out this attitude because in the end it will undermine our strategy.*

APPENDIX A

Glossary of Key Terms

Assimilator – a particular *reaction type* referring to an *outsider* who acquiesces to the expectations of the insider group by adopting the features and behaviors of the dominant culture and minimizing her/his "different" characteristics.

Avoider - a particular *reaction type* referring to an *insider* who is aware of biases in him-/herself and others, but is reluctant to counter the inappropriate words and behaviors of others and him-/herself.

Constructive Conversation - a particular type of conversation that either proactively or reactively addresses difficult, interpersonal issues. This type of conversation typically describes observations non-judgmentally and discloses emotional components as well as interpretation and meaning of behaviors.

Culture – behaviors and their meaning that are expected, reinforced and rewarded by and within a particular group.

Cultural Orientation – a particular culture-based value that forms the underpinning of behaviors and expectations.

Change Agent - a particular *reaction type* referring to an *insider* or *outsider* who is willing to take action when she/he encounters inappropriate words, behaviors or structures.

Diversity - variance and variability from a norm. In organizational terms, diversity refers to employees who do not conform to the established cultural norm. In a social context, the term *diversity* refers to the presence in one population of a wide variety of cultures, opinions, ethnic groups, socio-economic backgrounds, etc.

Diversity Dataset – a compilation of available statistical information about demographic and workforce trends in a given country or region.

Diversity Dynamic - the common social processes that underlie all diversity situations, regardless of whether they relate to gender, race, ethnicity, language, sexual orientation, age, organizational culture or any other source of differences.

Exclusion – a condition in which individuals or groups are not fully valued and integrated into a social context and culture.

Fighter - a particular *reaction type* referring to an *outsider* who actively and overtly resists the pressure to assimilate and opposes the restrictive expectations and norms enforced by the insider group.

Frame of Reference – A framework or system of meaning manifested by an individual in both the visible and invisible aspects of her/his being. This concept assumes that outwardly visible elements of an individual or a group are reflections of an internal set of attitudes, beliefs, assumptions, values etc. This framework is responsible for how an individual perceives, evaluates and relates to others.

Inclusion or Inclusiveness - a condition which allows variance and variability to exist and flourish. In organizational terms, inclusion refers to the climate and culture that allows employees who do not conform to the norm to flourish within the organization.

Inclusive Leadership™ - an umbrella term introduced by TMC to describe the skills and behaviors that realize inclusion, specifically *"setting and reinforcing standards for business practices that enable individuals and groups to contribute to their fullest potential by leveraging their unique abilities, experiences, perspectives and viewpoints for the collective benefit of all stakeholders."*

Inclusive Leadership Profile™ - an individual self-assessment of practices associated with inclusive leadership developed by TMC.

Insider/Outsider Dynamic or **Insider/Outsider Diversity Dynamic** - the common social processes that underlie all diversity situations, regardless of whether they relate to gender, race, ethnicity, language, sexual orientation, age, organizational culture or any other source of differences. Specifically, this dynamic recognizes a core dynamic between those with formal and/or informal power to establish standards, rules and norms (insiders) and those that have little or no power to set standards, rules and norms (outsiders).

Insiders – individuals and/or groups who have formal and/or informal power to establish standards, rules and norms.

Intentional Offender – a particular *reaction type* referring to an *insider* who is aware of her/his behavior and prejudices but, nevertheless, continues to exclude outsiders.

Outsiders - individuals and/or groups who have little or no power to set standards, rules and norms.

Reaction Types - a typology of behavioural strategies and patterns in interactions between *insiders* and *outsiders*.

Separatist - a particular *reaction type* referring to an *outsider* who limits contact with the dominant group.

Unintentional Offender - a particular *reaction type* referring to an *insider* who excludes and/or offends people in the organization because of their differences without being aware of it.

APPENDIX B

Recommended Resources

A suite of web tools and training solution publications have been developed to support the Cultural Orientations approach to building cultural competence.

1. The Cultural Navigator™

TMC's Cultural Navigator™ is the world's premier technology tool for cultural competence. Using a state-of-the-art web-based platform, the Cultural Navigator™ drives cultural awareness and reduces cultural risk by providing access to a wide range of learning, consulting and assessment solutions in one easy to understand, intuitive package. It represents a practical and powerful resource for individuals and clients interested in *improving their global effectiveness*.

The Cultural Navigator™ consists of seven primary channels:

Cultural Profile/Cultural Orientations Indicator (COI®) – the *only statistically validated online self-assessment tool available on the market* assesses individual cultural preferences and allows the user to apply the assessment results to a menu-driven comparative database of countries and regional profiles. Users can compare their personal cultural profiles with those of other cultures and identify areas of commonality as well as areas of cultural differences for which behavioral changes might be considered. Recommendations for behavioral changes are included with each individual profile.

CountryScope – a 100+ country database with a comprehensive cross-cultural comparison of management practices designed to enable users to adapt management styles for improved effectiveness. Recent upgrades to this channel include tabs for *Diversity, Relocation* and *Travel.* CountryScope content is also available for purchase directly through www.CountryScope.com (see below).

Learning Zone – provides access to TMC's blended learning solutions for Global Effectiveness, Leadership and Management Development. TMC's blended learning includes learning labs, virtual classes and coaching in addition to classroom learning, all designed to offer users a customized selection of delivery options to optimize individual learning.

Web Learning – direct access to TMC's flagship *Globalization* and *Cultural Orientations at Work* web courses.

Cultural Simulator - direct access to TMC's proprietary cultural simulations that allow users to test and reinforce awareness and learning by creating on-line simulations around a variety of management topics pertaining to a specific country or region.

Exchange - provides a platform for TMC's growing suite of Cultural Coaching Solutions, as well as creating a community for client users to offer comments and observations that add to the richness of the cultural experience available using the tool. TMC's expert coaches will moderate this feature and provide context and quality assurance.

Global Management Toolbox – a searchable database of InfoPacks™ containing information and tools on global management issues designed to improve cross-cultural management effectiveness.

Visit the Cultural Navigator™ at **www.culturalnavigator.com**

2. **www.CountryScope.com**
   TMC's newest web offering allows for access to real time, updated information on over 50 countries and regions in all parts of the world. Users can access information as CD-ROMs, downloads or licenses to streaming content.

   The information provided is fully integrated with the Cultural Orientations Model and provides a comprehensive introduction to the social and business culture of the specific country and region.

The following countries' information is available on www.countryscope.com:

Argentina, Australia, Austria, Belgium, Brazil, Canada, Chile, China, Colombia, Czech Republic, Denmark, Finland, France, Germany, Hong Kong, Hungary, India, Indonesia, Ireland, Israel, Italy, Japan, Malaysia, Mexico, Netherlands, Norway, Philippines, Poland, Russia, Saudi Arabia, Singapore, South Africa, South Korea, Spain, Sweden, Switzerland, Taiwan, Thailand, Turkey, United Kingdom, United States of America, Venezuela, Vietnam

In addition, the following regions are also available:

Asia/Pacific, Eastern Europe, Western Europe, Middle East and Africa, North America, Latin America

To order, visit www.countryscope.com or www.tmcorp.com.

3. **Management Navigator™ - TMC's web tool for management development**

The Management Navigator™ is a cutting edge web learning platform designed to help improve leadership and management effectiveness through the targeted identification of learning resources and management topics customized for today's global companies.

For more information on TMC's Management Navigator™, please contact TMC at +1.609.951.0525; or visit us online at www.tmcorp.com.

4. **Inclusive Leadership Navigator™**
This web-based portal provides users access to a variety of tools to develop or enhance their knowledge and skills as *Inclusive Leaders*. Such tools include:

- Inclusive Leadership Profile (ILP)™
- Information on key Diversity & Inclusion Topics
- Country and region specific *Diversity Profiles*
- *Diversity & Inclusion Simulator*

- *Best Practices and Leadership Tools*

Additional practical tools include:

- **Diversity and Inclusion Audit:** A tool that allows managers to assess their organization's needs with respect to its marketplace, talent (workforce), leadership, and policies and procedures. Contact TMC's Inclusive Leadership practice for details (www.tmcorp.com).

- **Diversity Reports:** Review of workforce and marketplace trends in over twenty countries. Topical reports on global trends.

Contact TMC at www.tmcorp.com for information on this and other Navigator tools.

5. TMC Learning Solutions for Global Effectiveness

TMC's Blended Learning Solutions extend the Cultural Orientations approach to specific domains of management. Each learning solution can be delivered face-to-face, virtually, or developed as a web-delivered program. Each topic is embedded with a thorough cross-cultural perspective and supports managers with global responsibilities:

- Cultural Orientations at Work
- Doing Business Globally
- Managing Across Cultures
- Managing Culture in Global Business
- Multicultural Teamwork
- Leading Global Teams
- Global Project Management
- Negotiating Across Cultures
- Presenting Across Cultures

In addition, country- and region-specific overview workshops are available and can be customized to an organization's learning needs.

APPENDIX C

Bibliography

Barak, Michàlle E. Mor. *Managing Diversity: Toward a Globally Inclusive Workplace.* London, UK: Sage Publications, 2005.

Berreby, David. *Us and Them: Understanding Your Tribal Mind.* New York, NY: Little, Brown and Company, 2005.

Cox, Taylor. *Cultural Diversity in Organizations: Theory, Research & Practice.* San Francisco, CA: Berrett-Koehler Publishers, Inc., 1994.

Goleman, Daniel. *Emotional Intelligence: Why It Can Matter More Than IQ.* New York, NY: Bantam Books, 1995.

Gladwell, Malcolm. *Blink: The Power of Thinking Without Thinking.* New York, NY: Little, Brown and Company, 2005.

Hayles, Robert and Arminda Mendez Russel. *The Diversity Directive: Why Some Initiatives Fail And What to Do About It.* New York, NY: McGraw-Hill, 1997.

Isaacs, William. *Dialogue: The Art Of Thinking Together.* New York, NY: Doubleday, 1999.

Klein, Janice. *True Change: How Outsiders on the Inside Get Things Done in Organizations.* San Francisco, CA: John Wiley & Sons, Inc., 2004.

Miller, Frederick and Judith Katz. *The Inclusion Breakthrough: Unleashing the Real Power of Diversity.* San Francisco, CA: Berrett-Koehler Publishers, 2002.

Prahalad, C.K. *The Fortune at the Bottom of the Pyramid: Eradicating Poverty Through Profits.* Upper Saddle River, NJ: Wharton School Publishing, 2005.

Rosenberg, Marshall. *Nonviolent Communication: A Language of Life*. Second Edition. Encinitas, CA: Puddle Dancer Press, 2003.

Schmitz, Joerg. *Cultural Orientations Guide: The Roadmap to Cultural Competence*. Fourth Edition. Princeton, NJ: Princeton Training Press, 2005.

Schmitz, Joerg. *Transcendent Teams*. Princeton, NJ: Princeton Training Press, 2001.

Stone, Douglas., et al. *Difficult Conversations: How to Discuss what Matters Most*. New York, NY: Penguin Books, 2000.

Stringer, Donna M. and Patricia A. Cassidy. *52 Training Activities for Exploring Value Differences*. Yarmouth, ME: Intercultural Press, 2003.

Stuber, Michael. *Diversity: Das Potenzial von Vielfalt nutzen- den Erfolg durch Offenheit steigern*. München, Germany: Luchterhand, 2004.

"The Hidden Wealth of the Poor: A Survey of Microfinance." The Economist. November 5th, 2005.

TMC Research Report: Population Aging: The Challenges Ahead. Princeton, NJ: Princeton Training Press, 2005.

TMC Research Report: Work-Life Balance: The Challenges Ahead. Princeton, NJ: Princeton Training Press, 2005.

TMC Research Report: The Disabled and Their Rights: An International Survey. Princeton, NJ: Princeton Training Press, 2005.

TMC Research Report: Gender: What it Means at Work. Princeton, NJ: Princeton Training Press, 2005.

Walker, Danielle, Tim Walker and Joerg Schmitz, *Doing Business Internationally*. Second Edition. New York, NY: McGraw-Hill, 2003.

Wind, Yoram (Jerry) and Colin Cook with Robert Gunther. *The Power of Impossible Thinking.* Upper Saddle River, NJ: Wharton School Publishing, 2005.

NOTES

1. According to the International Labour Organisation (http://www.ilo.org).
   Reference: Page 12

2. A useful tool that highlights important culture-based aspects of one's Frame of Reference is the Cultural Orientations Indicator (COI)®. This psychometrically valid assessment tool provides individuals with a comprehensive cultural profile. To learn more about the COI®, please visit http://www.tmcorp.com and click "Our Tools."
   Reference: Page 24

3. Note that this phrase does not refer to the adaptations and assimilation to common standards, work processes and practices that are justly required by any organization. We are referring largely to the tacit norms, standards, and expectations communicated in the workplace related to an individual's or group's background, experience, characteristics, lifestyle or values.
   Reference: Page 44

4. The Constructive Conversation Model is a synthesis of *Dialogue* by William Isaacs, *Difficult Conversations* by Douglas Stone, et al. and *Non-violent Communication* by Marshall Rosenberg, and Goleman (Emotional Intelligence). We have identified common aspects and conditioned them into a practical, five-step approach suitable for management interactions.
   Reference. Page 77

About the Authors

JOERG SCHMITZ serves as Director of Consulting and Learning Solutions at TMC, a global management and leadership consultancy headquartered in Princeton, New Jersey, U.S.A. He initiated and manages the *Cultural Competence, Global Teamwork* and *Inclusive Leadership* practice areas and supervises TMC's research and development activities in these areas.

Mr. Schmitz has designed and implemented consulting and education projects for numerous multinationals, including Schering AG, DaimlerChrysler, Hoffman La Roche, Johnson & Johnson, Pfizer, Citigroup, Corning, American Express, Infosys, Boehringer-Ingelheim, Merck, Merrill Lynch, Air Products and Chemicals, Young & Rubicam, ArvinMeritor and others. He is co-author of *Doing Business Internationally*, 2nd edition (2003, McGraw-Hill) and author of *Transcendent Teams* (2000, Princeton Training Press) and *The Cultural Orientations Guide* (1999, 2000, 2003, 2005; Princeton Training Press).

Mr. Schmitz is a cultural anthropologist trained in communication analysis and educated in his native Germany, in Mexico and the United States.

NANCY A. CURL managed the global diversity training programs for IBM from 2001 to 2005. During this time, she successfully launched *Shades of Blue,* a cultural training program, and *Diversity and Inclusive Leadership,* a program which focuses on leveraging our differences. Both programs use a blended learning approach with web-based modules that complement a learning lab. *Shades of Blue* won five citations for Excellence in Practice in 2002 from ASTD, a prestigious training organization in the U.S.A.

Prior to 2001, Nancy's experience was with the financial services line of business in IBM where she was a programmer, marketing representative, regional product manager, software product manager, customer requirements manager and, lastly, a global sector manager of Payment Systems in London, England.

Ms. Curl focuses on the use of a global framework, complemented by local population, trends, and legislative data, to link business impact to an inclusive environment. Nancy has conducted training sessions globally, including Japan, Singapore, India, Australia, Brazil, Argentina, Venezuela, Colombia, and throughout Europe to enrich the new program. Ms. Curl has worked in both Hong Kong and London for several years where she experienced personally the impact of diversity and cultural on business results. Ms. Curl continues to pursue her passion for this work as a consultant developing and delivering learning solutions.